THE
CLASSROOM TEACHER'S
INCLUSION
HANDBOOK

Other Books by Jerome C.Yanoff
The Classroom Teacher's Trouble-Shooting Handbook

Upcoming Books by Jerome C.Yanoff
The Classroom Teacher's Effective Teaching Handbook

THE
CLASSROOM TEACHER'S
INCLUSION
HANDBOOK

Practical Methods for Integrating Students with Special Needs

JEROME C. YANOFF

arthur coyle press
chicago, illinois

The Classroom Teacher's Inclusion Handbook

Arthur Coyle Press
P.O. Box 59435
Chicago, Illinois 60659-0435

Edited by Mary Edsey.

Printed in the U.S.A.
First printing 2000.

10 9 8 7 6 5 4 3 2

Publisher's Cataloging in Publication Data

Yanoff, Jerome C.
The Classroom Teacher's Inclusion Handbook / Jerome C. Yanoff
Includes 176 pages and index.
ISBN 0-9665947-1-1

1. Teachers
2. Inclusion
3. Special Education

371.9   99-093375

Contents

Introduction

During much of our nation's history the special needs of children who could not function in a regular classroom were largely ignored. There were no special programs for them. Schools discouraged them from attending or expelled them if they presented a hardship.

In the mid-1800s, through the efforts of such people as Thomas Hopkins Gallaudet and Alexander Graham Bell, some programs, most notably for the deaf, were established to teach children with special needs. By the turn of the century scattered programs served the special needs of only a small percentage of these children, but in the years following World War II about half were in special programs.

The first special education programs functioned apart from the regular classrooms, often in separate buildings. Teachers who worked with these students were called "special education teachers." Each teacher was trained in one area of special education, such as teaching the deaf or teaching the blind. The children were placed in or removed from the programs as administrators saw fit.

The current philosophy that all children, even those with special needs, have a right to an education grew out of the Civil Rights movement of the 1960s. Families who had children with disabilities realized that their children too were being denied a basic American right—public education.

In 1975 President Gerald Ford signed Public Law 94-142, the "Education for All Handicapped Children Act." Its most important provision insured that all children would be presented with a free and appropriate education in the least restrictive environment. The rights of special needs students were expanded under subsequent laws, particularly Public Laws 99-457 and 101-476 entitled the "Individuals with Disabilities Education Act" or "IDEA." They increased the amount of time and types of services students with special needs were able to obtain.

By the 1980s many parents and educators believed that students with special needs would learn better with their neighborhood friends in regular classrooms than in special classrooms with students who all had the same disability. To accommodate this new idea several states mandated that new teachers become acquainted with techniques for working with all types of special needs students. However, the required training (usually one survey course) provides only enough information to begin working with such students.

The Classroom Teacher's Inclusion Handbook continues that education with detailed information about each type of special need and practical suggestions for working with students who have them. The ideas in the book come from the author's 33 years of experience in the field of special education, both from his own teaching and from observing and working with others.

About the Author

Author Jerome C. Yanoff has taught special education in public school classrooms since 1966. He served for ten years as the union representative in his school and six years on the executive board of the Chicago Teachers' Union. He has been elected several times as a delegate to the Illinois Federation of Teachers and the American Federation of Teachers. He is currently teaching special education courses at several universities in the Chicago area.

How to Use This Book

The Classroom Teacher's Inclusion Handbook is an easy-to-follow book written for the regular classroom teacher. The first chapter includes an overview of inclusion and general information about all students with special needs. The fourteen chapters that follow are categorized by the specific mental or physical disabilities or exceptionalities of students. Some chapters are then subdivided into more specific types.

Each chapter or section begins with a definition of the disability or exceptionality. Most definitions listed are from Public Law 94–142. Named the *Individuals with Disabilities Education Act (IDEA)* in 1990, the law was first passed by the federal government in 1975 and has been amended several times since—most recently in 1997. This landmark legislation mandated special education in all public schools. It is the principle source for educators to define students with special needs. Other sources of definitions are used in some chapters in which a more concise definition was available.

Following the definitions, each chapter then lists by bullet point important facts, characteristic behavior, and suggestions for working with students with each type of special need. Because each disability or exceptionality presents unique problems, other topics, such as characteristic behavior of an undiagnosed problem, are also included when appropriate. Please note that in all sections, students who possess the problem being discussed may exhibit only one or several of the characteristic behaviors listed. To help the reader acquire further information, each chapter concludes with a list of reference books and web sites.

In an unusual situation the classroom teacher may receive specific instructions from a doctor, school nurse, special education teacher or parent concerning an individual student that oppose the suggestions in this book. If such a situation should occur follow the specific instructions given and not the suggestions in this book.

While using this book and learning more about students with special needs, it will become apparent that students with special needs are different from regular students. The differences may be very small or very large. Keep in mind that it is all right to be different, and you will be on the road to enjoying all your students— no matter what their differences may be.

Six Essential Elements for Successful Inclusion

1. The district sees inclusion as a program to serve children.

2. The principal sees inclusion as a way to better educate students.

3. The parents see inclusion as an opportunity for their child.

4. The teacher sees inclusion as a challenge and an occasion to promote growth.

5. The classmates see inclusion as a chance for personal development.

6. The student sees inclusion as an entrance to a more normal life.

Six Harmful Attitudes That Can Ruin Inclusion

1. The district sees inclusion as an opportunity to save money.

2. The principal sees inclusion as a way to save space in the school and punish uncooperative teachers.

3. The parents see inclusion as a way to confirm denial of their child's problems.

4. The teacher sees inclusion as an imposition and deviation from routine.

5. The classmates see inclusion as an opportunity to ridicule.

6. The student sees inclusion an environment of exposure and shame.

Chapter I

Inclusion

Definition

Inclusion is the practice of placing students with special needs in the regular classroom with non-disabled students and providing specialized services and/or curriculum for them.

The philosophy of inclusion is twofold: (1) children with special needs will develop better socially if they can attend classes with non-disabled children; and (2) children who are non-disabled will become more knowledgeable and sensitive when working with children who have disabilities.

Important Facts about Inclusion

- Though the terms "inclusion" and "mainstreaming" are sometimes used interchangeably, mainstreaming differs in that the special needs students placed in the regular classroom in this program receive the same education and services the other students are receiving.

- The procedure for placing a student in a special education program is regulated by federal law. When it becomes apparent that a student with disabilities cannot function in the regular classroom without receiving special education services, the parent, teacher or administrator, who feels the student requires special education services, initiates a multi-disciplinary conference, called a "staffing." Prior to the conference the student is tested in appropriate areas. At the conference parents and other adults involved with the student determine whether the student needs special education services. If so a plan, known as the Individual Education Plan (IEP), is made to provide the assistance the student needs. The IEP must include *(a)* the present educational abilities of the student, *(b)* the long range goals for the year, *(c)* the short range goals necessary to achieve the long range goals, *(d)* the specific educational support services to be provided by the school, *(e)* the extent, if any, of mainstream or inclusion participation, and *(f)* a method of recording progress in achieving the goals and objectives.

- The amount of extra work required of a teacher with a student with special needs depends on school regulations, the union contract, and the willingness and abilities of the teacher. A student with special needs appropriate for inclusion should fit into the class with minimal procedural alteration. Extra meetings, specialized training and special curriculum should be the responsibility of the special education teacher, not the classroom teacher. Additional paperwork, however, must be recorded by the classroom teacher: IEP information; changes in work and behavior; special reports and anecdotal material; changes in the student's medication; and additional record keeping, if the school employs a behavior modification program.

- The classroom teacher cannot and should not be expected to be a specialist in each area of special education, nor should parents and administrators demand it.

- If the classroom teacher feels good about inclusion, the special needs student will thrive. If the teacher feels resentful about the extra work, the student will suffer.

- Some students may be assigned an aid. The teacher is still in charge of the class and responsible for the student with special needs, even if the aid is older and has more experience working with children. The teacher and the aid should respect each other's expertise and work together.

- The number of special education students placed in one classroom depends on the type of disability each student has and the willingness of the teacher—there could be six special education students who require little additional help or one who is a constant handful.

- Though a regular classroom teacher cannot refuse to accept a student with special needs the teacher can refuse to perform certain services which are inappropriate for a teacher to do, such as, some medical procedures, toileting, lifting, feeding, etc.

- It is unlikely a classroom teacher would be sued if something goes wrong, if for no other reason than most teachers do not have enough money to make a legal suit worthwhile. It is more likely that a school board or school district would be sued.

- The number of students with special needs is increasing because *(a)* medical advances are saving the lives of children born prematurely, children with serious birth defects, and children affected by disease or serious accidents; *(b)* parents are responding to the option of educating their special needs children in public schools rather than special schools; and *(c)* edu-

3

cators are no longer allowing students with special needs, such as those with learning disabilities or emotional problems, to drop out of school, but are instead encouraging them to stay.

- Though the goals of inclusion are inarguably noble, in reality the system may present some difficulties. Administrators, school boards, teachers, parents and students must work together to ensure the program's success.

Suggestions for Working with a Student with Special Needs

- Acquire all the information you can about the student, including strengths and weaknesses, from the parents, special education teacher, administration, board of education and the student.

- Establish the reason for placing the student with special needs in your classroom. Make sure the reason is appropriate for the student.

- Though it is not necessary to attend an entire staffing for a student, you should be present when the student's IEP is being developed. The participants, particularly the parents, may have an unrealistic view of their child's abilities. You can provide a better perspective of what can and cannot be achieved based on the student's strengths and weaknesses, your capabilities, and the support available. If you cannot attend the meeting, ask to be briefed on the goals which were set and the reasons they were chosen.

- If the IEP goals seem unrealistic, request another meeting to set new goals. Do not let others make unreasonable demands of you and do not make unreasonable demands of yourself.

- Get a clear idea of the services expected of you. If you feel a responsibility is beyond your ability or inappropriate for you to perform, voice your reluctance before the student starts your class.

- Check with the union before refusing to perform any special services which seem inappropriate for a classroom teacher. If you are comfortable performing those services, do so.

- Discuss with the school administration and the union any legalities for working with the student with special needs.

- Based on the type of disability, the age of the children involved, and the desires of the student and parents, decide whether to prepare your class for the child's arrival. Some disabilities are immediately evident, others become evident as the school year progresses, and others are unnoticeable. Some disabilities, such as epilepsy, may be frightening and require the student's assistance in getting help. The parents of the child with the disability may want to come to school to talk to the class; the child may want to come along; the parents may prefer to have the teacher talk to the students; or the parents may prefer to keep the disability confidential. In any case, respect the parent's wishes. If the disability is to be discussed, ensure that the students receive a truthful representation of the new student and are allowed to ask questions and voice concerns. Encourage the class to accept differences and consider their classmate worthy of support and friendship, rather than attempting to minimize the student's problems.

- In most cases the student with special needs can and should be held to the same standards for classwork and behavior as the rest of the class. It is, rather, the support to achieve those standards that will require special service. In cases in which the disability excludes reaching normal expectations, the teacher must modify assignments, grades, behavioral demands, and the classroom, as necessary.

- Document the student's progress and failures.

- Accomplish the goals and objectives of the student's IEP to the best of your ability. Do as much as you and do the best that you can.

- Ask the special education teacher, the special education aid, and the parents of the student for suggestions about working with the student.

- If you feel a classroom aid is necessary request one. Enlist the help of colleagues, parents, administration and other students when necessary.

- If an aid is assigned to the student with special needs, work out the details of the daily class operation before the aid begins.

- If the relationship with the aid becomes difficult, maintain professional standards and avoid any action that would harm the aid's effectiveness. Expect the same from the aid.

- Always remember that you still have a class of regular students who also need your attention.

- If the placement of the special needs student is not working out, discuss the situation with the special education teacher and the school administrator. Get suggestions for better methods of working with the student. If the situation persists, request the administrator call another meeting to discuss a change of placement or services.

Glossary

Americans with Disabilities Act (1990) – Public Law 101-336 which extends civil rights to individuals with disabilities

at-risk – a type of student with a higher than average chance of developing a disability

disability – a limitation

due process – the right of families and schoolboards to get mediation in order to resolve disagreements about services to be provided for a student's special needs

exceptionality – a quality or situation which prohibits a student from receiving his educational needs in a regular classroom

handicap – a limitation imposed by the environment on a person who has a disability or by people's attitudes toward the disability

Individualized Education Plan / Program (IEP) – a program drawn up at a staffing to map out the delivery of special services to a special needs student

Individualized Family Service Plan (IFSP) – the plan developed to help nurture the abilities of children with disabilities from birth to age two

Individuals with Disabilities Education Act (IDEA) – Public Law 94-142 passed in 1975 with supporting legislation, most currently Public Law 105-17 in 1997, mandating the right of an appropriate education for all students regardless of their special needs

integrated classroom – a classroom that has both non-disabled and disabled students

interdisciplinary team – a group of educators from different areas, such as a regular classroom teacher, a special education teacher, a school nurse, a social worker, a psychologist, etc., who are responsible for developing an educational plan for a student with special needs

itinerant teacher – a teacher who does work in several schools, usually with special needs students

least restrictive environment – a situation as close in nature as possible to the regular classroom for a student with special needs

mainstreaming – a program in which students with special needs take classes in a regular classroom without receiving special services

multi-disciplinary conference / staffing (MDC / MDS) – a formal meeting of parents and educators at which a specific student's educational needs are discussed and a program developed to aid in the student's education

normalization – emphasis on conventional attitudes and behavior in the school setting for students with disabilities

paraprofessional – a person who works with the teachers and the students providing support services

pull-out program – a program in which a student is taken from the regular classroom to receive special help

Regular Education Initiative (REI) – the proposal that special education services be provided in the regular classroom with disabled and non-disabled students attending together

resilient child – a student who, in spite of a multitude of health and/or environmental problems, manages to cope beyond expectations

residential facility – a specialized school where the students live and attend classes

resource room – a special room in a school where a special needs student goes on a regular basis to get extra help with schoolwork

screening – a basic evaluation of a large group of students devised to locate those who may have a disability and will require further testing

Section 504 of the Rehabilitation Act (1975) – a part of law that provides that no otherwise qualified individual with a disability may be discriminated against in such places as school and work

special education – additional and specialized services given to students who would not be able to reach their potential in school without them

teacher aid – an adult assigned to provide support to a regular classroom teacher, a special education teacher, an individual student with special needs or a small group of students with special needs

Technology-Related Assistance to Individuals with Disabilities Act (1991) – a federal law which authorizes money to the states to set up a network for providing assistive technology to people with disabilities

transition services – services to help students with special needs adjust to work and living after finishing high school

zero reject – the principle which prohibits any student with a disability from being denied a free appropriate education

Reference Books

Gearheart, Bill R., Mel W. Weishahn, and Carol J. Gearheart. *The Exceptional Student in the Classroom.* 6th ed. Englewood Cliffs, NJ: Prentice-Hall, 1996.

Heward, William L. *Exceptional Children: An Introduction to Special Education.* 5th ed. Englewood Cliffs, NJ: Prentice-Hall, 1996.

Hunt, Nancy, and Kathleen Marshall. *Exceptional Children and Youth.* Boston, MA: Houghton Mifflin, 1994.

Meyen, Edward L. *Exceptional Children in Today's Schools.* 3rd ed. Denver, CO: Love Publishing Company, 1996.

Meyen, Edward L., and Thomas M. Skrtic, eds. *Special Education and Student Disability: An Introduction.* 4th ed. Denver, CO.: Love Publishing Company, 1995.

Smith, Deborah Deutsch, and Ruth Luckasson. *Introduction to Special Education.* Needham Heights, MA: Allyn and Bacon, 1995.

Turnbull, Ann, Rud Turnbull, Marilyn Shank, and Dorothy Leal. *Exceptional Lives: Special Education in Today's Schools.* 2nd ed. Saddle River, NJ: Prentice-Hall, 1999.

Web Sites

The Family Network Disability and Resource Link
gator.naples.net/presents/FamilyNetwork/disablink.html

Kids Together Inc.
www.kidstogether.org/inc.html

National Early Childhood Technical Assistance System (NEC-TAS)
www.nectas.unc.edu/

The National Information Center for Children and Youth with Disabilities (NICHCY)
www.nichcy.org

On Special Ed.Com
www.onspecialed.com/home.asp

Publishers of Special Education Material
www.cec.sped.org/fact/publisher.htm

U.K. Inclusion Site
www.inclusion.uwe.ac.uk/

Yours, Mine, Ours
www.jacksonville.net/~inclusion/

Chapter II

Students with Learning Disabilities

Definition

The term "specific learning disability" means a disorder in one or more of the basic psychological processes involved in understanding or in using language, spoken or written, which disorder may manifest itself in imperfect ability to listen, think, speak, read, write, spell, or do mathematical calculations. Such term includes such conditions as perceptual disabilities, brain injury, minimal brain dysfunction, dyslexia and developmental aphasia. Such term does not include a learning problem that is primarily the result of visual, hearing, or motor disabilities, of mental retardation, of emotional disturbance, or of environmental, cultural, or economic disadvantage.

—IDEA

Important Facts about Students with Learning Disabilities

- The term "learning disabilities" applies to a wide range of problems in the areas of oral expression, listening comprehension, written expression, basic reading ability, reading comprehension, mathematical calculation and mathematical reasoning, and the cognitive processes of perception, attention, memory, metacognition and organization. Learning disabilities may affect one of these areas or many in varying ranges of severity.

- Learning disabilities can be detected by testing students who are having academic problems. The two tests most often given are the *Illinois Test of Psycholinguistic Abilities (ITPA)* and the *Marianne Frostig Developmental Test of Visual Perception (Frostig)*.

- About 51 percent, by far the largest percentage, of students receiving special education services are categorized as learning disabled.

- The ratio of boys to girls with learning disabilities is three to one.

- The incidence of certified learning disabilities varies from state to state and district to district because there is no standard criteria for granting special education services.

- Although neurological and genetic effects are widely explored as the source of learning disabilities, the causes are generally unknown and may be numerous.

- Unlike other disabilities, learning disabilities are more likely to be discovered by a teacher than by a parent because many learning processes are first applied in school.

- There is no such thing as a profile of a student with learning disabilities. The only commonalities are the students' frustration and lack of academic achievement.

- A child with a learning disability does not achieve at a level appropriate to age or ability.

- Many students with learning disabilities also have problems in developing social and behavioral skills.

- Learning disabilities are often difficult to discover in a student because the student has developed the ability to avoid answering questions and to guess correctly from contextual clues.

- There is often a behavioral overlay with students that have learning disabilities. It is largely due to the frustration of not understanding or to the inability to work at the same rate as other students.

- A student with learning disabilities misses social cues the same way learning cues are missed and, therefore, often has problems developing social skills.

- Students with learning disabilities, whether they graduate or not, often remain at entry level positions in the workplace.

- The educational prognosis for students with learning disabilities is not good. Many drop out because of frustration with their inability to do the work, lack of desire to produce the additional effort, or lack of social success.

Characteristic Behavior of Students with Learning Disabilities

- Exhibit a discrepancy between ability and performance (the most revealing characteristic).

- Achieve at an uneven rate, sometimes years apart, from one area of learning to another (the second most revealing characteristic).

In reading

- Have difficulty in oral reading.

13

- Have poor comprehension in silent reading.
- Read slowly.

In writing
- Spell poorly with some words very badly misspelled.
- Use vocabulary below age level.
- Have poor handwriting.
- Make numerous mistakes when copying.

In speaking
- Forget names of people and familiar objects.
- Use the wrong word to name or explain something.
- Respond inappropriately.
- Mix up word order.
- Do not understand when to talk and when to listen in conversations.

In math
- Lack the ability to apply calculating processes consistently.
- Copy numbers inaccurately.
- Have difficulty interpreting word problems.
- Have difficulty distinguishing pertinent from unnecessary information.

In thought processes
- Have poor memory.
- Have difficulty generalizing.
- Have difficulty putting information in sequence.
- Have difficulty retrieving answers or words from memory.
- Have poor concept of time.
- Confuse right and left.
- Judge distance poorly.

In classroom procedures

- Frequently guess at answers.

- Do not complete work.

- Are disorganized and messy.

- Often lose materials needed for classwork.

- Do not show signs of understanding when work is explained.

- Have difficulty following directions.

In self-esteem and behavior

- Feel stupid.

- Have low frustration tolerance.

- Have a negative attitude.

- Display avoidance behavior.

- Engage in acting-out behaviors.

- Have poor social skills with resulting low social acceptance.

- Misinterpret social cues.

In body movement

- Lag behind in developing fine muscle coordination.

- Lack rhythm of movement.

Characteristic Behavior of
Students with Undiagnosed Learning Disabilities

- Exhibit uneven academic performance.

- Exhibit discrepancy between work and ability.

- Display several avoidance behaviors.

- Become increasingly disinterested in school.

Suggestions for Working with a
Student with Learning Disabilities

Because there is such a wide variety of learning disabilities, it is important to discuss the student with the special education teacher or consultant and work out an individualized plan of action. Use the following suggestions as a general reference.

In classwork

- Focus on strengthening skills rather than helping to complete a specific assignment.
- Have the student work with computer programs specifically designed for students with learning disabilities.
- Arrange for group and peer tutoring.
- Arrange with parents to tutor their child at home.

In reading

- Provide high interest material.
- Make sure the student knows the sound of each letter and letter blends. Practice word attacks.
- Suggest that the student place a ruler or straightedge under the line being read to help keep place.
- Have the student read a paragraph and then paraphrase it.
- Develop questions for the reading selection in which the reader must understand the feelings of the character. Ask the student to project likely reactions.
- Ask if the student would like to read aloud but do not insist on it. If possible give the student the reading assignment the day before to practice.
- Periodically have choral reading with the entire class.

In writing

- If the student is having trouble writing, suggest using a thicker pencil or pen.
- Allow the student to keep a chart of letters and numbers to check writing accuracy.
- Provide writing exercises with adequate repetition.
- Dictate short sentences for the student to write that are already

printed on the student's paper but covered over. Have the student compare what he wrote with what you wrote on the paper.

- Help the student develop outlines for assigned reports.
- Allow the student to work with a classmate when doing a classroom writing assignment.
- Allow enough time to finish. Do not insist that work be handed in when the allotted time is up.
- Teach the student to use a computer keyboard and give assignments which can be done on the computer.
- Have the student keep a journal.

In mathematics

- Develop calculator skills.
- Allow the student to use multiplication and division charts.
- Use manipulatives when teaching new concepts.
- Teach the student to pay attention to math signs.
- Help the student to analyze story problems and convert the words into math symbols.
- If possible reduce the number of drill problems the student must do.
- Focus on step-by-step procedures for math problems. Provide the student with a model that has numbered steps.
- Allow the student to work with another student or group.
- Allow the student to finish work at home.

In academics

- Break large assignments into several small assignments.
- Provide the student with an outline of the lesson.
- Teach the student how to find the topic sentence in each paragraph.
- Write significant material on the chalkboard.
- Teach the student how to take notes.
- Allow the student to tape-record lessons and lectures.

- Allow the student to work with other students who can help with some of the basic study and work procedures.

In test-taking

- Give the student fewer problems.

- Give the student additional time.

- Give the tests orally.

- Allow the student to take the test in a different setting.

- Read the directions to the student and have the student paraphrase the directions as they are read.

- Allow the student to answer questions speaking into a tape recorder.

In perception

- Have plastic or cloth letters and numbers for a young student. Let the student trace the letters and numbers with her finger. Have the student practice making the shapes on paper. Have the student walk in an open space to make the shapes of the different letters and numbers.

- Have the student use manipulatives whenever possible.

- Provide concrete examples of different objects discussed in class.

In attention

- Have the student sit in the front of the class. If the student is not paying attention, stand near the student.

- Develop a cue such as "now listen to this" whenever there is something you want the entire class to pay attention to. Train the class to recognize its importance.

- Give only one or two directions at a time.

- Bring the entire class to attention before making a transition from one task to another.

In memory

- Help the student to associate concepts with concrete examples.

- Provide written step-by-step instructions for assignments with multiple steps.

- Provide mnemonic devices, such as "HOMES" for remembering the Great Lakes (Huron, Ontario, Michigan, Erie, Superior), or develop them with the student.

In metacognition

- Develop a program of self monitoring, i.e., every five minutes the student charts what he is doing at that moment (listening, talking, day-dreaming, working, playing, etc.).

- Teach the student to listen and follow directions.

- Have the student develop a method for working with problems or tasks and see that the method is followed.

- Encourage the student to verbalize methods of doing assignments.

In organization

- Color code each subject using different color folders and matching textbook and workbook covers.

- Be sure that the student is putting away papers in the correct folders or in the proper place in his notebook.

- Have the entire class check on personal supplies every Friday afternoon. Develop a checklist that everyone can use.

- Check to see that all assignments are written in an assignment notebook. Sign the notebook at the end of the day. Have a parent sign the book when the homework assignment is done.

- Have the student check to see that all the necessary books and supplies are packed in the schoolbag before going home. Have the parent check the bag before the student leaves for school in the morning.

- Have the student end each day by cleaning and organizing his desk.

In behavior and sociability

- Assure the student he is not stupid but has a different way of learning.

- Acknowledge the difficulty of learning the academic tasks.

- Let the student know that help is available.

- Acknowledge work which has been completed.

- Praise success and accomplishment.

- Keep a folder of successful work.

- Teach the student to accept responsibility for his behavior.

- If it is necessary to punish, make the punishment immediate, logical and rehabilitative.

- Do not allow the student to be teased for his disability.

- Have the student work with a group of two or three other students.

- Teach the student how impulsive behavior affects others.

- Train the student to think about an answer instead of giving an answer impulsively.

- Discuss options in social situations.

- Analyze missed social cues.

- Discuss yielding to peer pressure.

- Provide for and encourage healthy peer interactions.

Glossary

discrepancy – a difference between ability and performance

dyscalculia – a learning disability in mathematics

dysgraphia – a learning disability affecting handwriting

dyslexia – a learning disability in recognizing and/or comprehending written words

encoding process – the ability to organize information so it can be learned

generalization – the ability to apply what is learned to other settings

metacognition – the ability to monitor and evaluate how we are performing

perception – the ability to organize and interpret what is experienced through the senses

Reference Books

Deshler, D., and K. Lenz. *Teaching Adolescents with Learning Disabilities: Strategies and Methods.* Denver, CO: Love Publishing Company, 1996.

Reid, K. *Teaching the Learning Disabled: A Cognitive Developmental Approach.* Boston, MA: Allyn and Bacon, 1988.

Smith, S. *No Easy Answers.* New York, NY: Bantam Books, 1995.

Web Sites

The Daily Apple
  thedailyapple.com

Hello Friend/Ennis William Cosby Foundation
  www.hellofriend.org

International Dyslexic Society
  www.interdys.org

L.D. Online
  www.ldonline.org

Learning Disabilities Association (LDA)
  www.ldanatl.org

Learning Disabilities Professional's Directory
  www.iser.com

PACE
  pacetutoring.com/learning-disabilty.htm

Chapter III

Students with Behavior Disorders and Emotional Disturbance (BD/ED)

- *Students with Aggressive Behaviors*
- *Students with Withdrawn Behaviors*

Definitions

Emotionally disturbed is a condition exhibiting one or more of the following characteristics over a long time and to a marked degree that adversely affects a student's educational performance: an inability to learn that cannot be explained by intellectual, sensory, or other health factors; an inability to build or maintain satisfactory interpersonal relationships with peers and teachers; inappropriate types of behavior or feelings under normal circumstances; a general pervasive mood of unhappiness or depression; a tendency to develop physical symptoms or fears associated with personal or school problems. —IDEA

The term "emotional or behavioral disorder" means a disability that is (i) characterized by behavioral or emotional responses in school programs so different from appropriate age, cultural, or ethnic norms that the responses adversely affect educational performance, including academic, social, vocational or personal skills. Such a disability (a) is more than a temporary, expected response to stressful events in the environment, (b) is consistently exhibited in two different settings, at least one of which is school related, and (c) is unresponsive to direct intervention in general education or the child's condition is such that general education interventions would be insufficient. (ii) Emotional and behavioral disorders can co-exist with other disabilities. (iii) This category mat include children or youth with schizophrenic disorders, affective disorders, anxiety disorders, or other sustained disorders of conduct or adjustment when they adversely affect educational performance in accordance with section (i).

—Steven R. Forness and Jane Knitzer

(Although schizophrenia is considered a type of emotional disturbance, it is more appropriately included in Chapter XII – Students with Severe and Multiple Disabilities.)

Important Facts about Students with BD/ED

- School districts use different terms to categorize students with behavior disorders and emotional disturbance. Matching each word from the left column with each word from the right column enumerates most of the terms used.

behaviorally	disturbed
emotionally	impaired
socially	handicapped
personally	maladjusted
	disordered
	conflicted

- Though special education programs may group students with emotional disturbance and students with behavior disorders together, the two are quite different. Behavior disorders refer to conditions characterized by aggressive anti-social behavior. Emotional disturbance refers to problems developed due to poor parenting, poor coping skills and stress. Although students with behavior disorders are often harder to control in the classroom, students with emotional disturbance are generally harder to treat.

- The characteristic behavior of children with behavior disorders or emotional disturbance is vague and imprecise. It is therefore necessary for teachers to use their professional judgment when deciding if a student should be screened for these conditions. The intensity, duration, frequency, and age appropriateness of a student's behavior should be considered.

- The teacher would be notified if a student is diagnosed with BD/ED. These medical and psychiatric diagnoses are made by doctors and clinicians and should never be made by a classroom teacher.

- The school counselor, special education teacher, parents, school nurse, or family doctor may provide specific instructions for working with a student with BD/ED. Instructions of this kind should take precedence over the more generalized suggestions listed in this text.

- If a student exhibits the characteristics of a behavior disorder or an emotional disturbance but the behavior does not interfere with schoolwork, the student may require outside help but does not need special education services.

- Although some emotional disorders are physiological, it is still possible to modify and control behavior.

- The teacher's main task is to present the educational material. Modifying behavior is secondary.

- Treatment of emotional disorders is based on two schools of thought:

    1. the psychoanalytic model (developed by Sigmund Freud) assumes that the disorders are a result of conflicts in the unconscious and that treatment depends on uncovering and resolving these conflicts; and

    2. the behavioral model (developed by B.F.Skinner) assumes that the disorders result from faulty learning and that treatment depends on controlling the environment to teach more appropriate responses.

- Working with students with behavioral disorders and emotional disturbance is significantly different than working with children with other disabilities because *(a)* there is no need to modify the work; *(b)* students play an active role in the severity of the disability; *(c)* the teacher can play a role in the improvement of the disability; *(d)* as difficult and disruptive as the students are capable of being, if they become connected to the teacher they are equally capable of being loyal and protective; *(e)* teachers can exert control on the frequency and extent of the student's problems; *(f)* parents are not necessarily allies in helping their children improve; *(g)* the teacher must separate the student as a person from the behavior; *(h)* the variety of behaviors and symptoms is vast; *(i)* the degree of the disorders is difficult to quantify; and *(j)* the student is capable of drawing the teacher into the disability.

- Students with BD/ED are sometimes holding in large amounts of anger and frustration. When this erupts it can result in destruction to property and harm to self and others. Often the students are frightened of becoming out of control and begin to leave clues in hopes that an adult will discover them and help them get under control again.

Characteristic Behavior of Students with BD/ED

- View the world and surrounding events only in relation to themselves.

- Will go to great lengths to avoid what is unpleasant.

- Engage in self-defeating behaviors.

- Manipulate others to achieve own ends.

- Make poor personal choices.

- Lack insights into personal problems.

- Often choose short-term solutions over long-term solutions.

- Require immediate gratification.

Characteristic Behavior of Students with Undiagnosed BD/ED

- Lack interest in school and schoolwork.

- Do not complete schoolwork.

- Have poor relationships with peers.

- Argue with adults.

- Behave inappropriately for age group.

- Exhibit absent, inappropriate or frequently intense feelings.

- Lack interest or concern for others.

- Repeat unnecessary movements.

- Are frequently truant.

- Are frequently anxious.

- Insist on perfection.

- Obsess over seemingly minor problems.

- Show poor grooming and health habits.

- Avoid others.

- Frequently misbehave.

- Are frequently the center of trouble though appearing not to be a part of it.

- Frequently complain and make negative comments.

- Are frequently the subject of complaints and negative comments from classmates.

- Overemphasize or lack emphasis of self.

- Frequently complain of physical ailments.

Students with Aggressive Behaviors

Characteristic Behavior of Students with Aggressive Behaviors

- Argue.

- Lack control.

- Become easily frustrated.

- Have tantrums.

- Set fires.

- Tease and provoke others.

- Steal.

- Swear.

- Interrupt.

- Fight.

- Are often disruptive.

- Bully other students.

- Engage in power struggles.

Suggestions for Working with a Student with Aggressive Behaviors

- Be firm in providing structure.

- Be clear about expectations.

- Be patient and calm during outbursts.

- Do not be afraid to confront a student about inappropriate behavior.

- Be fair and logical in giving consequences.

- Have the student work with other students who are not easily intimidated.

- Model good behavior.

- Inform the student when behavior is inappropriate and review what the appropriate behavior is.

- Do not get angry unless you are the target or the victim of an inappropriate act. If this is the case, get angry and explain to the student the results of his action. Condemn the action but not the student.

- Try not to get involved in power struggles unless there is a safety factor involved. It is better to model good behavior than to try to force the student to perform it.

- Work on improving social skills.

- Compliment appropriate behavior.

- Assign responsibilities.

- Assure the student of individual worth and value to the class.

- Maintain high expectations.

- Avoid being drawn into the student's personal life. Arrange for the student to meet with the school counselor if the student often attempts to discuss personal problems.

- Do not take personally any statements that the student has made in anger.

- Avoid acting on behalf of the student or doing special favors.

- Do not feel fear, anger, pity or vengefulness toward the student.

Students with Withdrawn Behaviors

Characteristic Behavior of
Students with Withdrawn Behaviors

- Are quiet in class and shy toward others.

- Prefer to be left alone.

- Seem fearful.

- Appear unhappy.

- Lack energy.

- Are overly anxious.

- Often unable to focus.

- Exhibit obsessive and compulsive behaviors.

- Are frequently absent.

- Make self-depreciating remarks.

- Inflict injury on themselves.

- May be suicidal.

Suggestions for Working with a Student with Withdrawn Behaviors

- Insist on good work.

- Be clear in your expectations.

- Assign classroom responsibilities.

- Help the student develop social skills.

- Be warm and accepting. Make the student feel a sense of worth.

- Have the student work with another student or a small group of non-threatening students.

- Protect the student from being teased or belittled.

- If the student becomes overly depressed, allow the student to retreat to a private part of the room or put her head down on the desk until able to rejoin the class. Do not insist that the work be completed at these times but hold the student accountable for completing the work later. Notify the parents and the school counselor if depression is frequent, and initiate a plan to manage it.

- If a student threatens or mentions suicide or murder, immediately *(a)* talk to the student about the enormity of the topic, and insist on the value of living, *(b)* discuss the importance of the student to you and the class, *(c)* bring the student to the school counselor, and *(d)* notify the administration and the student's parents. Do this even if the student insists it was only meant to be a joke.

- If a student makes any statement threatening destruction, ques-

tion the student and report the statement to the school counselor and the student's parents.

Definitions of Specific Types of BD/ED and
Suggestions for Working with a Student Who Has Them

adjustment disorder – a maladaptive reaction to a stressful situation which disappears when the stress is removed

- Offer the student support during times of stress.

- Talk him through what he is doing while getting him to focus on
  the exact nature of the stress.

- Give positive feedback when the situation is resolved.

aggression – an act of disregarding the safety and rights of others
in order to promote one's own desires

- Insist that the behavior will not be permitted in the school.

- Insist that the student return inappropriate gains made.

- Enforce the required consequences.

- Help the student find other, more socially acceptable ways to
  gain desired ends.

anorexia – severe self-starvation

- Because this is a very difficult disorder to work with, get
  instructions from the parents or family doctor.

anxiety disorders – a set of disorders, including phobias, panic
attacks, obsessive/compulsive disorders, and post traumatic stress
disorder, in which the student feels an unnecessary amount of
fear, worry or uneasiness about doing everyday activities.

- Be flexible. Do not insist that the student always act in the
  same manner as the rest of the class.

bipolar disorder – severe mood swings which go from mania
(extreme excitement) to depression (previously called "manic-
depression")

- Get instructions from the parents or family doctor on what to do if the student goes into a severe mania or depression.

- Expect to help control the mania but not the depression.

- Expect the student to stay home when the condition becomes severe.

bulimia – reoccurring binge eating followed by purging (often related to anorexia)

- Get instructions, if available, from the parents or family doctor.

character disorder – acting-out, aggressive disorder in which the student shows little or no regard for others and no feelings of guilt for having done something wrong

- Refer to the suggestions on aggressive behaviors.

conduct disorder – repetitive persistent patterns of behavior which violate or endanger others, such as inflicting harm on animals or other people, destroying property, lying, stealing and habitually breaking school rules.

- Refer to the suggestions on aggressive behaviors.

depression – depressed mood with loss of interest and lack of pleasure in daily activities

- Try to involve the student in activities with others.

- Encourage the student to take pleasure in accomplishments. If depression becomes too strong, allow the student to withdraw for periods of time with supervision from the school counselor or special education teacher.

encopresis/enuresis –incontinence of bowels and urine

- Insist on receiving a specific plan from the student's parents or family doctor before accepting the student in your classroom.

impulsivity – the inability to delay gratification and the tendency to act without thinking or considering the results

- Help the student to consider consequences.

- Insist that the student return inappropriate gains made through impulsivity.

- Enforce the required consequences.

- Place the student in situations where thinking before acting is required.

mania – excessive love or enthusiasm centered on a particular activity or subject

- If the mania is inappropriate, intercede by forbidding the student to act out the mania.

- Enforce the required consequences.

- Request directions from the family doctor or the special education teacher.

mood disorders – disorders of emotion, elation or depression that dominate one's outlook on life

- Try to teach and model appropriate moods for the activity in progress.

- Encourage the student to express appropriate feelings.

obsessive / compulsive disorder – a pattern of repetitive, persistent and intrusive thoughts (obsessions) and actions (compulsions) which interfere with the daily activities of a person's life

- Try to accommodate these actions if not too intrusive or disruptive to classroom procedure.

- Work with the student to limit the amount of disruption caused.

oppositional defiant disorders – a pattern of negative hostile behavior in which a student defies authority and school rules and may deliberately act in a way to annoy others

- Try to reach the student with positive reinforcements for appropriate behaviors. (If the student feels invested in the teacher, it is possible for the teacher to request, teach and reward more appropriate behaviors.)

panic attacks – an overwhelming irrational fear causing heavy shallow breathing, sweating, rapid heartbeat, and retreat from the feared stimulus

- Stay close to the person having the panic attack and give assurance that the feared object will not cause harm.

personality disorders – maladaptive behaviors related to perceiving and thinking about oneself in relation to the environment, which result in poor functioning and personal failure and distress

- Expect the student to be very difficult to work with.
- Consult often with the special education teacher and the family doctor.
- Remember that the student may not be choosing to act in self-defeating ways.
- Use punishment judiciously.

phobias – irrational and unwarranted fears

- Try to help the student deal with or overcome the phobia by helping the student approach the fear, understand it, and act appropriately.
- Do not try to force the student to do this.

pica – the eating of non-food objects such as hair, paint chips, or cloth

- Offer the student something more desirable to eat if the student will forego the pica.

post-traumatic stress syndrome – a reaction to an extremely threatening incident after which the student experiences sleep disorders, eating disorders, anxiety and avoidance behavior to a degree that interferes with daily life

• Request specific instructions from the special education teacher or family doctor on how to help the student.

• Avoid putting the student under additional stress.

• Try to involve the student in as much daily classroom activity as possible.

psychopath (anti-social personality disorder) – a person who exhibits amoral and anti-social behaviors such as hitting, stealing, lying, etc., with impulsive, irresponsible, self-serving ends and little or no regard for others

• Set very clearly defined consequences, inflexible in their execution, for inappropriate behavior.

• Watch the student closely.

• Remove the student from class if the behavior becomes too much of a problem.

psychosexual disorders – any disorder involving sexual functioning or sex-typed behavior

• If appropriate, monitor the student's behavior with a clearly defined set of expectations and consequences.

• If an infraction occurs remove the student from the regular classroom.

• Make sure the standards for the student's behavior are defined with the well-being of the students in mind and not personal philosophies.

school phobia – fear of going to school usually accompanied by anxiety, physical complaints and tiredness

• Try to make the student comfortable in school as well as going to and from school.

• If necessary let the student express fears and concerns about attending.

- If possible recommend that a program be established to bring the student to school on days when it is difficult to come voluntarily.

separation anxiety disorder – a fear of being separated from the parent (usually the mother), which is common the first few days of school until the child becomes accustomed to being away from the parent (in some cases the anxiety is strong and is felt by both the student and the parent).

- Engage the student in activities and the problem often goes away by itself.

- If the child and the parent are sharing the anxiety insist that the parent leave the area and let the student cry or carry out a tantrum until ready to join the class.

- If the problem persists notify the school counselor.

Tourette's syndrome – a neurological disorder characterized by motor and vocal tics, such as sudden movements or shouted words (sometimes obscene), sometimes accompanied by learning disabilities, attention-deficit/hyperactive disorders, obsessive/compulsive disorders and sleep disorders

- Seat the student away from distractions.

- Provide the student with a study carrel if necessary.

- Allow the student to leave the classroom to go to the bathroom or a safe place if the tics become excessive.

- Do not allow classmates to tease the student.

Glossary

behavior modification – a method of shaping behavior by rewarding wanted responses and ignoring or punishing unwanted responses

contingency contracting – an agreement that performing or giving up specific behaviors will result in an agreed reward

DSM-IV (Diagnostic and Statistical Manual of Mental Disorders, 4th ed.) – the manual developed by the American Psychiatric Association for classifying emotional disturbances

egocentric – a view of all things in relation to oneself

modeling – giving a demonstration of a desired behavior

projective test – a test, such as the Rorschach Test (ink blots) or the Thematic Aperception Test, in which responses are determined by experiences and state of mind

socialized aggression – aggressive and disruptive behavior learned and performed in a group setting, such as gang activity

tic – a sudden involuntary spasmatic movement or utterance

Reference Books

Kauffman, J.M. *Characteristics of Emotional and Behavioral Disorders of Children and Youth.* New York, NY: MacMillan, 1993.

Kerr, M.M., and C. M. Nelson. *Strategies for Managing Behavior Problems in the Classroom.* Columbus, OH: Merrill, 1983.

McDowell, R.L., and F. A. Wood. *Teaching Emotionally Disturbed Children.* Boston, MA: Little, Brown and Co., 1982.

Mendler, A.N. *How to Achieve Discipline with Dignity in the Schools.* Bloomington, IN: National Education Service, 1992.

Web Sites

Healthier You, a Mental Health Resource
www.mhsource.com/healthieryou.htm

National Institute of Mental Health (NIMH)
www.nimh.nih.gov

Chapter IV

Students with Attention-Deficit/ Hyperactivity Disorder
(AD/HD)

- *Students with Predominantly Inattentive Type AD/HD*

- *Students with Predominantly Hyperactive-Impulsive Type and Combined Type AD/HD*

Definition

The essential feature of Attention-Deficit / Hyperactivity Disorder is a persistent pattern of inattention and / or hyperactivity-impulsivity that is more frequent and severe than is typically observed in individuals at a comparable level of development (Criterion A). Some hyperactive-impulsive or inattentive symptoms that cause impairment must have been present before age 7 years, although many individuals are diagnosed after the symptoms have been present for a number of years (Criterion B). Some impairment from the symptoms must be present in at least two settings (e.g., at home and at school or work) (Criterion C). There must be clear evidence of interference with developmentally appropriate social, academic, or occupational functioning (Criterion D). The disturbance does not occur exclusively during the course of a Pervasive Developmental Disorder, Schizophrenia, or other Psychotic Disorder and is not better accounted for by another mental disorder (e.g., a mood disorder, Anxiety Disorder, Dissociative Disorder, or Personality Disorder (Criterion E).

— American Psychiatric Association

(Reprinted with permission from the *Diagnostic and Statistical Manual of Mental Disorders*, Fourth edition. Copyright 1994 American Psychiatric Association.)

Important Facts about Students with AD/HD

- Attention-deficit/hyperactivity disorder is a medical diagnosis. This diagnosis should never be made by a teacher.

- The words "hyperactive" or "hyper" are overused and misused. A child can be overactive without being hyperactive.

- Children with AD/HD, as children with other disabilities, have limitations. They are not choosing to act the way they do.

- Children with AD/HD can be very frustrating for a teacher to work with. Although it may seem that they are testing the teacher's structure to see what they can get away with, they are not. They too are unhappy with their behavior but cannot always control it.

- About 20 percent of children with AD/HD also have some form of learning disability. About 33 percent of children with AD/HD also have some form of behavior disorder. About 35 percent of children who are seeing a therapist on a regular basis are being treated for AD/HD. This represents the largest percentage of all childhood psychological disorders.

- About 20 percent of children with AD/HD have problems with depression or anxiety.

- Children with AD/HD are highly imaginative and creative.

- Children with AD/HD try harder in school when they feel the teacher likes them.

- Problems with AD/HD cannot be resolved but can be eased.

- A behavioristic program is more effective than a psychotherapeutic program.

Suggestions for Working with a Student with AD/HD

- Give only one or two instructions at a time.

- Have the student repeat instructions aloud.

- Talk through academic processes, such as mathematical procedures. Teach the student to do this alone.

- Color code the students textbooks, workbooks and folders by subject.

- Allow the student to keep a set of textbooks at home.

- Help the student make transitions from one subject to another by limiting transition time.

- Have the student write all homework assignments in an assignment book. Review and sign the book at the end of the day and have a parent sign the book at home.

- At the end of each day allow a few minutes for all the students to organize their desks and work.

- Set a routine and try to stay with it. Prepare the student for exceptions.

- Use behavioral contracts that specify the amount of time allotted for activities.

- Alternate highly interesting and less interesting tasks.

- Favor visual presentations over audio.

- Teach keyboard skills.

- Give the student rewards such as computer time and free reading time rather than candy.

- Allow the student to move around the room if it can be done without disturbing others.

- Help the student to understand inappropriate behavior.

- Give a lot of feedback.

- Do not become exasperated or display frustration.

- Communicate frequently with the parents.

Students with Predominantly Inattentive Type AD/HD

Characteristic Behavior of Students with Predominantly Inattentive Type AD/HD

- Often appear to be daydreaming or staring.

- Are often confused about what to do.

- Appear apathetic and unmotivated.

- Seem slow-moving.

- Make many careless mistakes.

- Show reluctance to engage in tasks which require commitment.

- Are unassertive, polite and docile.

- Attempt to bond with other students, but few respond.

Suggestions for Working with a Student with Predominantly Inattentive Type AD/HD

- Seat the student in close proximity with others.

- Assign a study-buddy to work with the student.

- Assign as much group work as possible.

- Stand near the student's desk during some of your presentations.

- Make eye contact during verbal instruction.

- Use introductory phrases to important information, such as

"Now I want everyone to be certain to pay attention to this."

- Ask the student to repeat instructions back to you.

- Try to call on the student when the student is paying attention. Give positive feedback for correct answers.

- Provide the structure and support necessary to do the work.

- Allow extra time to complete work.

- Write assignments on the chalkboard as you give them. Leave them on the board for a while.

- Break large assignments into smaller assignments.

- Try to apply the same academic standards as those for the rest of the class but be prepared to be flexible.

- Teach the student to monitor behavior.

- Make the student feel comfortable about asking for help.

Students with Predominantly Hyperactive-Impulsive and Combined Type AD/HD

Characteristic Behavior of Students with Predominantly Hyperactive-Impulsive and Combined Type AD/HD

- Often fidget and squirm.

- Often get out of seat.

- Display excessive physical activity.

- Are bossy and irritating and do not play well with others.

- Cannot play or work quietly.

- Talk excessively.

- Burst out with answers before the question is finished.

- Have difficulty awaiting turn.

- Interrupt.

- Act rude.

- Fail to pick up social cues.

- Show off.
- Are rebellious and short-tempered.
- Act immature.
- Have frequent emotional outbursts.
- Have poor organizational skills.
- Often forget or lose assignments.
- See events in black or white.
- Have poor self image.

Suggestions for Working with a Student with Predominantly Hyperactive-Impulsive and Combined Type AD/HD

- Assign the student a seat on the periphery of the class near the front, but away from the windows.
- If necessary provide a separate seat in a relatively empty part of the room where the student may sit whenever necessary. Supply the desk with a complete set of books and essential supplies. Erect partitions which seclude the desk from the rest of the class. Teach the student to record his own behavior with periodic checks (i.e., once every five minutes).
- Allow the student to get up and mark completed assignments on a wall chart.
- Assign tasks that require the student to move around the room or building.
- Teach relaxation techniques.
- Assign activities that can be done in pairs. Then pair the student with a strong well-organized partner.
- Look for areas where the student can appropriately provide leadership.
- Stress cooperation over competition.
- Practice social amenities.
- Acknowledge good work.

- Use positive reinforcement as much as possible.
- Use positives and praise, more than negatives and punishments.
- If necessary develop alternate ways to access progress.
- Provide immediate feedback on work and behavior.
- Provide the student with a list of classroom rules.
- Ignore minor inappropriate behaviors.
- Do not punish behavior that cannot be controlled.
- Help the student through transitions.
- Never take away recess or PE as a consequence.
- If spelling is particularly difficult assign five to ten words each night.
- Have the student practice writing words in the air.
- In math help the student align columns.
- In math give handouts and rely less on copying.
- Allow the use of calculators.

Important Facts about Medication for Students with AD/HD

- Ritalin and Cylert are the most commonly prescribed medications for AD/HD. Dexedrine is prescribed less often. Each is a stimulant that has a reverse effect of calming (depressing) the children who take them. A smaller number of children are prescribed anti-depressants.
- Doctors start children off with a weak dosage. If no improvement is shown, the dosage will slightly increase until there is a change in behavior.
- Children usually receive counseling with the medication.
- The most common side effects of medications taken for AD/HD include insomnia, decreased appetite, stomach pains, increased heart rate, and irritability.
- About 30 percent of children who try medication for AD/HD respond negatively. Some have no response at all.

- The parents and family doctor will usually ask the teacher to monitor changing behavior in a child who is beginning to take medications.

- The teacher should be informed of all changes in medication.

- Whether to give medication to children with attention deficit disorders is a controversial topic.

- Some adults feel that medicating such children demonstrates the parents' desire to control their child's behavior with an easy fix. They feel the child would be better served if the parents learned to deal with the child's behavior.

- Other adults feel that such children would be unreachable both at home and at school were it not for the medication they take.

- Whether to give medication to a child is a family decision that should not involve the teacher. The role of the classroom teacher is to lend support to the parents who must make this difficult decision.

- The classroom teacher should never suggest to parents that their child needs medication.

Glossary

Cylert – a stimulant given to reduce hyperactivity

Dexedrine – an amphetamine used to reduce hyperactivity

hyperactivity – the quality of having excessive energy and movement, much of which may be out of control

impulsivity – the quality of acting on a thought before thinking out the consequences

Norpramin – a depressant used in treating hyperactivity

psychotropic medication – medication which alters feelings, behavior and perception

Ritalin – a stimulant used to reduce hyperactivity

Tofranil – a depressant used in treating hyperactivity

Reference Books

Dendy, C.A.Z. *Teenagers with ADD: A Parents' Guide*. Bethesda, MD: Woodbine House, 1995.

Hartman, T. *Attention Deficit Disorder: A Different Perspective*. Lancaster, PA: Underwood Miller, 1993.

Lerner, Janet, Barbara Lowenthal and Sue Lerner. *Attention Deficit Disorder: Assessment and Teaching*. Pacific Grove, CA. Brooks/Cole Publishing.

Reif, Sandra. *How to Reach and Teach ADD/ADHD Children*. Upper Saddle River, N.J.: Prentice Hall, 1994.

Web Sites

Children and Adults with Attention Deficit Disorders (CHADD)
www.chadd.org

National ADDA
www.add.org

Chapter V

Students with Autism

- *Higher-Functioning Students*
- *Lower-Functioning Students*

Definition

Autism means a developmental disability significantly affecting verbal and nonverbal communication and social interaction, generally evident before age 3, that adversely affects educational performance. Other characteristics often associated with autism are engagement in repetitive activities and stereotyped movements, resistance to environmental change or changes in daily routine, and unusual responses to sensory experiences. The term does not apply if a child's educational performance is adversely affected primarily because the child has a serious emotional disturbance.

—IDEA

Important Facts about Students with Autism

- Autism manifests itself in a variety of ways and a range of severity. Some autistic children require constant support because they behave in bizarre ways, such as being out of control, or being unable to listen or respond to others. Others require only minimal support because they behave in just a slightly odd way, such as speaking with unusual intonation.

- Higher functioning people with autism perform normally in making friends, marrying, and maintaining a job.

- About 75 percent of autistic children are boys.

- Very few people with autism have the savant syndrome (previously called "idiot-savant").

- Because it limits the ability to communicate, autism is sometimes viewed as a communication disorder.

- Autism most likely has a physiological basis and not a psychological basis, as was previously thought.

- Because children with autism may be very difficult to maintain in the regular classroom, the classroom teacher should be expected to do only the best she can under the circumstances.

- No matter how difficult a student with autism may be, the child still feels joy and pain like any other child.

- The teacher, the autistic child and the aid should take delight in all successes and not feel overly frustrated or guilty about academic goals not reached.

- Many schools have a substantial support network for children with autism which includes the special education teacher, social worker, speech-language therapist, occupational therapist and other adults.

Characteristic Behavior of Students with Autism

- Function best in an environment of routine and predictability.
- Respond to everyday events unpredictably.
- Become easily frustrated and upset.
- Throw tantrums in response to frustration.
- Prefer to be alone.
- Dislike being touched.
- Lack eye contact and have little awareness of other's presence.
- Become fixated on certain objects.
- Prone to sudden self-destructive violence when upset, such as head-banging, biting or scratching. May also damage the room or harm others, though not intentionally.
- React adversely to certain sounds, such as the hum of a fluorescent light, or to certain textures, such as some clothing fibers.
- Engage in self-stimulating behaviors, such as hand flapping, rocking, twirling, self-hitting, etc.
- Develop islets of competence in one or more of the following areas: perfect musical pitch, skill in drawing, memory of statistics, mental math.
- May have exceptional memory for trivial matters.
- Confuse pronouns.
- Recite phrases repeatedly that were just heard (echolalia).
- Engage in little or no speech. Some may communicate with sign language or use facilitated speech.
- Typically have an I.Q. substantially lower than normal people, but may possess any level of intelligence including genius.

Higher-Functioning Students

Suggestions for Working with a Higher-Functioning Student with Autism

- Be more concerned with the student's social interactions than with schoolwork.

- Work out a grading system that reflects the progress made by the student. Discuss this with the administration and the student's parents.

- If appropriate assign the student a study-buddy to help organize, do class assignments and note work to be done later.

- If the student can cooperate, encourage working in groups.

- Emphasize developing communication skills.

- Help the student learn to verbally express feelings of discomfort.

- Provide the student with a daily schedule. If there are to be any changes to the schedule, inform the student as soon as possible and assure the student that the day will be all right.

- Provide the student with a list of rules which must be followed.

- Give the student two sets of books, one for home use and one for school use.

- Break down assignments into small isolated steps. When one step is mastered go to the next step.

- Provide guides and examples for any assignments the student finds too difficult.

- Gradually increase the number of tasks the student is to perform.

- Emphasize visual presentations of classwork rather than spoken presentations.

- Emphasize computer and keyboard skills.

- Highlight important written information.

- Present real-life situations.

- Teach to the student's strengths.

- Do not punish the student for behavior that cannot be controlled.

- If possible acquire the services of an aid to help the autistic student with organization and daily functioning.

- Consider scheduling the student for speech and language therapy.

- Recommend occupational and vocational therapy for older students.

Lower-Functioning Students

Suggestions for Working with a Lower-Functioning Student with Autism

- Establish the reasons the student is being placed in your room.

- Request the services of a one-on-one aid who will be responsible for maintaining the daily functioning and appropriate behavior of the student.

- Request that the student not be sent to school if the aid is absent. Do not accept a substitute aid.

- Inform the parents if you are planning to be absent from school.

- Periodically review the student's behavior and progress with the aid. Do not be afraid to constructively critique each other.

- With your administration and the student's parents work out a grading system which will reflect the achievements the student has made.

- Do not make completing classwork or keeping up with learning a primary goal.

- Concentrate on providing functional curriculum.

- Encourage interaction between the student and classmates.

- Include the student in as many classroom activities as the student is able to handle.

- Establish a routine.

- Avoid overwhelming the student. Either show the student what is to be done or tell the student, but do not do both at the same time. The student may be able to tolerate only one set of stimuli at a time.

- Make directions as concrete as possible. Show pictures if you can.

- Break down assignments into small isolated steps. When one step is mastered go to the next step. Do not let unfinished assignments accumulate.

- Develop communication skills through spoken language, communication boards, sign language or any combination of these.

- Capitalize on fixations by using them as rewards or transitions for learning. Do not try to remove them.

- Try to replace stereotypical behaviors (hand flapping, rocking, etc.) with more appropriate behavior and forms of communication.

- Try to replace acting-out and self-destructive behavior with other forms of communication.

- Demand, but do not always expect, age-appropriate behavior.

- Praise all successes.

- If the placement is not working out, ask the administrator to call another staffing to alter the original plans or change the student's placement.

Suggestions for Handling an Outburst

- Do not feel that an occasional outburst makes the student unacceptable in a regular classroom. Students with autism can be taught to change their behavior.

- With the help of the parents and the aid determine a plan to handle outbursts, particularly those that are physical. The plan should be aimed at helping the student regain control and should not be punitive. Establish when the plan should be implemented. Advise the student of the plan.

- Request that the parents commit to picking up the student from school anytime the student seems unable to control his behavior for the day.

- Try to determine the cause of the outbursts, especially if there are several, by either asking the student or by trying to analyze the events preceding the outburst. If possible, remove the cause.

- If the student becomes agitated as a result of having broken a rule have the student read the rule aloud, several times if necessary.

- If the student appears to be getting agitated over a classroom activity, give the student another activity or, if necessary, move the student to a safe place.

- If the student feels he is becoming upset and can express this, or if the teacher or aid feel the student is becoming upset, have the aid remove the student to a safe place. If the student is capable of writing what is bothering him, have him do so.

- Remove the student from outside stimulation.

- Calm the student with as little touching as possible.

- Do not allow the student to injure himself or any other person in the classroom. Use restraining as a last resort.

- Teach relaxation techniques to the student.

Glossary

Asperger Disorder – a disorder in which a person has many of the behaviors associated with autism but not the language delays or cognitive impairments

echolalia –the parroting of words or phrases usually immediately after they are heard

echopraxia – the automatic and meaningless repetition of a movement which was just observed

facilitated communication – a procedure using a communication board which enables many with limited or no communication ability to have some communication (the degree of success will vary with the individual)

perseveration – persistent repetition of a verbal or motor response

pervasive developmental disorder – a disorder which impairs several facets of life including communication, behavior, social interactions, and learning

savant syndrome – the ability to memorize trivial facts or be able to perform unimportant mental tasks despite generally lower mental functioning

stereotypical behavior – persistent repetition of an action or speech pattern

Reference Books

Fullerton, Ann, Joyce Stratton, Phyllis Coyne, and Carol Gray. *Higher Functioning Adolescents and Young Children with Autism.* Austin, TX: PRO-ED, 1996.

Williams, Donna. *Autism: An Inside-Outside Approach.* London: Kingsley, 1996.

Web Sites

The Autism Society
   www.autism.org

Chapter VI

Students with Mental Retardation

- *Students with Mild Mental Retardation*
- *Students with Moderate Mental Retardation*

Definition

Mental retardation refers to substantial limitations in present functioning. It is characterized by significantly subaverage intellectual functioning, existing concurrently with related limitations in two or more of the following applicable adaptive skill areas: communication, self-care, home living, social skills, community use, self-direction, health and safety, functional academics, leisure, and work. Mental retardation manifests before age 18.

—American Association on Mental Retardation

(Reprinted with permission of the American Association on Mental Retardation, 1992.)

There are four sub-categories of mental retardation:

1. mild – I.Q. 50 to 70 to 75; educable mentally handicapped (EMH) or educable mental retardation (EMR); require support services in school, work and home living (includes about 85 percent of people with mental retardation);

2. moderate – I.Q. 35 to 50; trainable mentally handicapped (TMH) or trainable mentally retarded (TMR); require extensive support services and supervision in school, work, and home living (includes about 10 percent of people with mental retardation);

3. severe – I.Q. 20 to 35; require extensive support and supervision; and

4. profound – I.Q. under 20; require support and extensive care in all aspects of their lives.

The I.Q. ranges included in this section are meant to serve only as a reference and not as a solitary factor in determining the sub-categories. There are other rating scales which are also used to evaluate the abilities of these students.

This section discusses only students with mild or moderate retardation. Severe and profound retardation are included in Chapter XII – Students with Severe and Multiple Disabilities.

Important Facts about Students with Mental Retardation

• Mental retardation can be an entity unto itself or part of a syndrome. Some disorders which may have mental retardation as a component, but do not necessarily include it, are Down Syndrome, Fragile X syndrome, spina bifida, phenylketonuria (PKU), Tay-Sachs disease, cerebral palsy, galactosemia, hydrocephaly, microcephaly, Duchene muscular dystrophy, Turner syndrome, Klinefelter syndrome, Prader-Willi syndrome, fetal alcohol syndrome, Rett syndrome and Raye syndrome.

- Although many people picture a child with mental retardation as a Down syndrome person, most people with mental retardation appear normal.

- The term "mental retardation" cannot be the sole determinant of a student's ability. Students with mental retardation possess a wide range of abilities.

- A teacher should view the student's abilities, not his limitations.

- Children with mild and moderate retardation are aware they are not as smart as everyone else. It is important for the teacher to acknowledge their achievements and increase their self-esteem.

- A teacher may feel guilty about advancing to the next topic and leaving a student behind, if the student with mental retardation is not grasping the concept. However, if both the teacher and the student are trying as hard as they can, they should both feel successful about any progress being made.

Characteristics Behavior of
Students with Mild and Moderate Mental Retardation

- Possess limited social skills.

- Behave immaturely.

- Become easily frustrated.

- Lack self-confidence.

- Exhibit need for a lot of support.

- Tend to withdraw.

- Often forget self-maintenance and grooming tasks.

- Lack motivation.

- Are often sick.

- Display some stereotypical behaviors.

- Lack age-appropriate language skills.

- Function substantially lower in academic work.

- Exhibit poor metacognition skills.

- Are usually unable to think abstractly.

- Don't retain information for long periods of time.

- Have a short attention span.

- Have difficulty in skill transference.

Students with Mild Mental Retardation

Suggestions for Working with a Student with Mild Mental Retardation

In general classroom procedures

- Include the student in all classroom activities.

- Assign classroom duties.

- Work at the student's skill level instead of the class's skill level.

- Try to keep assignments similar or related to what the rest of the class is doing.

- Give short assignments.

- Provide an outline of the lessons.

- Allow the student to highlight passages in the textbook.

- Help the student keep books and papers organized.

- Teach keyboard skills and allow the student to work and play games on a computer.

- Use repetition.

- Use mnemonics.

- Relate the class lesson to real-life experiences and skills.

- Say the student's name to attract his attention before asking a question.

- Pair with a study-buddy.

- Praise frequently, but only when earned.

- Work out a separate grading system with the school administration and the student's parents.

In language arts

- Develop writing skills.

- Teach the spelling of basic words.

- Improve handwriting.

- Improve reading skills and encourage reading for pleasure.

- Encourage silent reading.

- Stress language skills.

In mathematics

- Work on the four operations. Use concrete examples and manipulatives.

- Teach calculator skills.

- Use real-life situations and story problems.

- Teach skills in using money.

In social studies

- Teach an awareness of the community and its services.

- Teach how to use public transportation to get around the community.

In physical education

- Teach good eating habits.

- Teach personal maintenance skills and physical fitness.

- Develop gross and fine-motor skills.

- Insist on age-appropriate play at recess.

Students with Moderate Mental Retardation

Suggestions for Working with a Student with Moderate Mental Retardation

In general classroom procedures

- Ensure that the goals set for the student are realistic.

- Request help from either a special education teacher or an aid.

- Develop plans with the parents so work can be reinforced at home.

- Give assignments that are both shorter and easier to do than those given to the rest of the class.

- Break down assignments into components. Give one at a time.

- Give concrete rather than abstract examples.

- Allow the student to speak answers and assignments into a tape recorder.

- Provide the student with study sheets which require filling in blanks.

- Do not put the student into too many situations where choices have to be made.

- Reduce distractions.

- Work on daily living skills (functional curriculum).

- Work on social skills.

- For group work, assign the student to a specific group and a specific role within the student's capabilities.

- Develop an alternative method of grading.

- Work on developing vocabulary and communication skills.

- Insist that classmates treat the student as an equal member of the class.

- Protect the student from being teased.

- Include the student in as many classroom activities as possible.

In language arts

• Work on word attacks for reading.

• Work on building reading comprehension.

• Teach reading for information and pleasure.

• Increase spoken and written vocabulary.

In mathematics

• Teach skills for shopping.

• Teach skills for managing personal finances.

• Teach how to tell time both on an analog and digital watch.

• Teach skills needed on a job.

In social studies

• Teach about the resources in the community and where to go for specific kinds of help.

• Teach how to use public transportation to get around the community.

Additional Areas of Functional Curriculum for a Student with Mild or Moderate Mental Retardation

In job training

• Teach how to apply for a job and how to fill out a job application form.

• Teach skills that will be needed on a job.

• Teach how to follow a work schedule.

• Teach how to cope with problems that may arise on the job.

• Teach social skills for working with others.

In personal care

• Teach grooming.

• Teach personal hygiene, cleanliness and nutrition.

• Give instructions on what to do when ill.

- Teach about love relationships.

In independent living

- Give instructions and practice for keeping clean living quarters.
- Teach how to shop for food.
- Teach how to prepare food.
- Teach how to use appliances and utilities in the home.
- Teach how to handle emergencies.

In leisure time

- Introduce the student to various leisure time activities.
- Help the student develop appropriate friendships.

In behavior and social skills

- Demand age-appropriate behavior.
- Teach the student the rules of the room and insist they be followed.
- Develop a number of tasks the student can do in the classroom.
- Provide opportunities for the student to interact with classmates.
- Encourage the parents of classmates to invite the student to birthday parties and other out-of-school activities.

Alternative Ways of Testing a Student with Mild or Moderate Mental Retardation

- Test-taking for students with mental retardation is an area of major adjustment. Some students may find tests threatening because they know they cannot do well. Others will feel ashamed because they are given a different test or are not being tested. The teacher has several options: *(a)* give the regular test, *(b)* give the regular test but grade it differently, *(c)* give the regular test orally, one on one, *(d)* give a shorter version of the test, *(e)* allow the test to be taken at home, *(f)* give an entirely different test, *(g)* give the test and allow the student to do it with help from an aid, *(h)* give additional time to finish, and *(i)* give an alternate assignment instead of giving the student a test. These modifications should be made only for those students who need them. Modifying the test for the entire class in an attempt to make the student with mental retardation feel better is a disservice to the entire class.

- For younger students, the teacher should choose the option which will most benefit the particular student. For older students, the teacher may pick two or three options and ask the student to decide which provides the most rewarding situation.

- Some students with retardation may ask to take the same test everyone else is taking. Although the student most likely cannot pass the test, the self-esteem gained in the attempt may outweigh the benefits of passing an easier test. In this situation the student should be praised for trying hard.

Glossary

anencephaly – a condition in which the brain is either absent or not completely developed

developmental disability – a mental or physical disability developed in childhood which is likely to be permanent

epicanthic fold – the flap of skin over the innermost corner of the eye which is characteristic of children with Down syndrome

functional curriculum – a curriculum which focuses on developing skills in communication, self care, home living, community living, socialization and job skills

generalization – the ability to apply what is learned to other settings

job coach – a person who works on a job site helping employees with limited skills do the work and become integrated into the workplace

learned helplessness – a condition in which a person expects to fail and, instead of trying, learns to depend on someone else or do without

life-skills curriculum – (see functional curriculum)

sheltered workshop – a facility which provides employment with close supervision for those who are unable to work well independently

stereotypical behavior – persistent repetition of an action or speech pattern

task analysis – the breaking down of complicated complex tasks into smaller components which are easier to teach

trisomy 21 – the most common cause of Down syndrome, which indicates a third chromosome attached to the twenty-first gene pair

Reference Books

Cronin, Mary E., and James R. Patton. *Life Skills Instruction for All Students with Special Needs.* Austin, Texas: PRO-ED, 1993.

Edwards, Jean, and David Dawson. *My Friend David; A Source Book about Down Syndrome and a Personal Story about Friendship.* Austin, TX: PRO-ED, 1983.

Guralnick, Michael J., ed. *The Effectiveness of Early Intervention.* Baltimore, MD: Paul H. Brookes, 1997.

Kaufman, Sandra Z. *Retarded Isn't Stupid, Mom.* Baltimore, MD: Paul H. Brookes, 1988.

Meyers, R. *Like Normal People.* New York: McGraw–Hill, 1978.

Web Sites

The ARC of the USA
www.thearc.org/welcome.html

The National Down Syndrome Society
www.ndss.org

Chapter VII

Students with Giftedness and Talents

- *Students with Giftedness*
- *Students with Talents*

Definitions

The term "gifted and talented" when used in respect to students, children or youth means students, children or youth who give evidence of high performance capability in areas such as intellectual, creative, artistic, or leadership ability, or in specific academic fields, and who require service or activities not ordinarily provided by the school in order to fully develop such abilities.

—Public Law 103-382 - Title XIV (1988)

Giftedness and talent is an overlapping of above average ability, creativity and task commitment brought to bear upon general or specific performance areas.

—J. S. Renzulli

(Reprinted with permission from *Phi Delta Kappan*, Vol. 60 , No. 3, p.180. Copyright 1978 Joseph S. Renzulli.)

Though it can be argued that every student has some gift or talent, this chapter will discuss only those who are exceptionally gifted and talented, using the following terms:

1. *giftedness* – high intellectual ability and an I.Q. at least two standard deviations above the norm (the 130 to 135 range);

2. *talents* – unusually high ability in athletics, leadership or the arts.

Important Facts about
Students with Giftedness and Talents

- Students who are gifted and talented usually find the regular classroom to be limiting. They are capable of going far beyond their peers. The regular classroom cannot provide them with the learning opportunities they need to maximize their abilities. This is what makes them special education students.

- Students who are gifted and talented are the only group of special education students who do not have federally mandated programs. The federal government encourages the states to set up programs for them, but the final decision rests with the school districts and the states, who base their decisions on the availability of revenue and the pressure of local activists.

- Gifted and talented programs are lacking due to the attitude that bright students can take care of themselves. Though this is true, the philosophy of American education is that each student be given the opportunity to reach his or her limits. Therefore, lack of gifted programs does not meet this philosophy.

- Every American high school has at least two programs for the gifted and talented—the boys' football team and the boys' basketball team. It is not wrong to have these programs, but it is not enough.

- American educators are often critical of the fact that other industrial nations do not pay enough attention to their most difficult students. Americans, however, don't pay enough attention to the most productive students.

Students with Giftedness

Definition

Giftedness is a combination of greater awareness, greater sensitivity, and greater ability to understand and transform perceptions into intellectual and emotional experience.

—Annemarie Roeper

(Reprinted with permission from *The Roeper Review*, November, 1982, Vol. 5, No.2, p.8-10. Copyright 1982 The Roeper Review.)

Important Facts about Students with Giftedness

- Statistically only one person in 1,000 has an I.Q. of 137 or higher, and only one person in 1,000,000 has an I.Q. of 160 or higher.

- There are 47 states who have adopted definitions for "giftedness." They are all different but tend to follow that of P. L. 103-382.

- Many districts do not have programs for gifted students. The responsibility then falls on the shoulders of the classroom teacher. In the worst case scenario, the classroom teacher does nothing to meet the special needs of gifted students. In the second worse case scenario, the classroom teacher tries to supply an appropriate program for the gifted student all by herself.

- A good student should not be confused with a gifted student.

The gifted student may or may not be a good student. The good student will create consistently good work, but the gifted student has the potential to produce concepts, ideas, programs and projects. If the teacher can meet the potential of this student, there is a good chance the potential will be reached.

- Americans generally have a love-hate relationship with the gifted. They enjoy knowing about exceptionally brilliant people, but don't appreciate them personally, and often resent them.

- Gifted girls often have difficulty displaying their intelligence. They are frequently taught that it is not good to be too smart, because people won't like them and boys won't ask them out on dates. They learn it is better to be quiet and keep their gifts to themselves.

- Gifted boys are more likely than gifted girls to be placed in special programs, receive one-on-one help and encouragement, and receive additional services from both male and female teachers.

- Americans put a great deal of emphasis on I.Q. scores. I.Q. scores merely predict a student's capabilities in school. Some schools use I.Q. scores as the sole determinant for special programs; others refuse to use them at all.

- Gifted students are not gifted in all areas.

- Gifted students are capable of seeing the world in different terms than their classmates and even their teachers. They tend to see people and events in a more integrated and more dynamic way and are able to view the future as well as focus on the present.

- The belief that gifted people are prone to emotional problems is a myth. On the contrary, gifted people have a better chance of finding healthy ways to cope in life than average people. Their often nonconformist thinking and behavior may cause others to consider them unusual or eccentric, but they are seldom harmful or destructive.

- Teachers receiving a gifted student frequently expect a model student and are disappointed to find that the student is more often challenging and demanding. If the teacher meets these challenges and demands, she may have a model student. However, if the teacher tries to make the student conform to the rest of the class, the student will quickly become oppositional and disruptive, and the teacher will find she has a highly skilled adversary.

- Gifted children are more often found in upper and middle class neighborhoods than in working class neighborhoods because

  1. high academic ability may be more highly regarded in upper and middle class neighborhoods than in working class neighborhoods,

  2. middle and upper class families are more likely to nurture giftedness and have resources to do so, and

  3. schools in upper and middle class neighborhoods have higher expectations for their students, and

  4. students in working class neighborhoods are more likely to hide their giftedness from their peers.

Characteristic Behavior of Students with Giftedness

- Accomplish grade-appropriate work with ease.

- Have a mature vocabulary.

- View learning with pleasure.

- May slide along just to get by with work but will not forsake interest in learning.

- Are always filled with ideas; are creative, inventive.

- Are always highly curious.

- Have a propensity to organize information.

- Usually emerge as the organizer and the leader of a group.

- Have a good memory.

- Become deeply involved.

- Look for additional work.

- Are intense.

- Have the ability to do abstract thinking.

- Can evaluate what has just been learned.

- Understand the interrelatedness of knowledge.

- Understand the relationship between themselves and the world.
- Have the ability to see a problem from more than one side.
- Have the ability to produce multiple solutions.
- Have a broad understanding of problems.
- Are energetic in attacking problems.
- Can provide rational explanations in all areas.
- Have assuredness about solutions.
- Are modest about accomplishments.
- Take it for granted that they are correct.
- Have the ability to generate more questions.
- Have preference for conversing with older people.
- May prefer books or computers to friends.
- Spend large amounts of time with other gifted students.
- Are unusually sensitive to others.
- Have a strong sense of fairness and justice.

Suggestions for Working with a Student with Giftedness

- Do not be intimidated by a child with a high I.Q. (A 10-year-old child with an I.Q. of 150 has the mental intelligence of a 15-year-old and does not have the life experience and general knowledge of the teacher.)
- Teach the student the value of his gift.
- Teach the class to value the gift of the student.
- Be flexible. Teaching a gifted student can be a good learning experience for both the student and teacher.
- Keep your expectations for the student high.
- When working in groups, place bright students together to provide them all with a more challenging environment.
- Arrange for the student to take some classes with older students in higher grades.

- If any teacher has a skill in an area of the gifted student's strength, see if a connection can be made with that teacher and the gifted student.

- With the parents look for out-of-school programs and opportunities in the community where the student can apply and expand his skills.

- Encourage the student to enter competitions.

- Incorporate the student's areas of expertise into other areas of study.

- Compress more than one year's work into the year.

- Avoid holding back appropriate work because it is supposed to be done next year.

- Do not push the student ahead too hard or too fast. Be aware of resistance.

- Give the student projects rather than individual assignments (i.e., if each student is learning about an individual European country have the gifted student devise her own project with European geography).

- Reduce the amount of drill for accuracy (i.e., if the class is doing 50 multiplication problems have the gifted student do only the first five and last twenty).

- Avoid giving inappropriate work to the student. (Although it is easy to say that it won't hurt a gifted student to do work that is too easy, the fact is that it wastes the student's school time.)

- Do not become upset or demanding if the student finds a way of doing work different from the way you taught. If the student's way is not good, it will soon be discovered.

- Do not make the gifted student a junior helper or tutor. Many gifted students do not like this nor should they be expected to.

- Do not insist the student work on exercises which have no personal value.

- Do not try to push the student in a particular direction.

- Do not force social skills on the student. Do not be concerned if social life becomes neglected in favor of intellectual life.

- Do not assume that the student's emotional maturity matches his intellectual maturity.

- Do not assume that the student has leadership abilities.

- Allow the student to engage in age-appropriate activities.

- Be sensitive to any feelings of isolation or loneliness the student might develop.

- Promote extracurricular activities in your school.

- Promote programs for the gifted in your district.

Students with Talents

Definition

The talented are those who excel in human endeavors. Though "talented" is a term often used interchangeably with "gifted," this text uses the term to describe those students who possess a high level of ability in non-academic areas.

Important Facts about Students with Talents

- Students who are talented have a need to develop their talents. The school has a duty to provide for this. A young athlete should not be held back from participating in sports because of her poor work in algebra any more than a budding mathematician should be held back from algebra because of poor performance of PE exercises.

Characteristic Behavior of Students with Talents

- Possess a skill level surpassing those of their peer groups.

- Spend an inordinate amount of time in their area of expertise.

- Often lose track of time when engaged in their field.

- Engaged in their field for the love of it rather than the promise of any reward.

- Interested and informed about other people in their field of interest.

Suggestions for Working with a Student with Talents

- Support the student's pursuit of excellence.

- Ask the class to support the student by attending events in which the student is participating.

- Allow the student to take some classes with another teacher who has a similar talent.

- Allow the student to incorporate talents with other classwork.

- Help the student select school activities and community programs which will enhance the skill.

- Be flexible with the student's schedule to allow the student time to participate in activities.

- Do not push the student too hard or too fast.

- Do not make a reward or punishment of the talent.

- Do not make the student feel the area of talent is not as important as other types of schoolwork.

Glossary

acceleration – presenting curriculum in a shorter period of time

compacting – reducing the amount of standard work and replacing it with enrichment work

conceptualization – the ability to formulate original ideas

convergent thinking – reaching a conclusion through known facts and thinking skills such as memory and reason

creativity – a type of intelligence marked by divergent thought bringing forth original ideas

differentiated curriculum – a curriculum which is flexible to allow independent and accelerated learning

divergent thinking – reaching a conclusion through creativity, flexibility and originality

enrichment – adding material to a topic to give it greater breadth and depth

magnet school – a specialized school which brings together students from many areas to pursue a common curriculum

Reference Books

Coangelo, N., and G. A. Davis, eds. *Handbook of Gifted Education.* Boston, MA: Allyn and Bacon, 1997.

Galbraith, J. *The Gifted Kid's Survival Guide.* Minneapolis, MN: Free Spirit Publishing, 1983.

Van Tassel-Baska, J. *Planning Effective Curriculum for Gifted Learners.* Denver, CO: Love Publishing Company, 1992.

Winner, E. *Gifted Children.* New York, NY: Harper Collins, 1996.

Web Sites

The ERIC Clearinghouse on Disabilities and Gifted Education
www.ericec.org

Gift Links
www.cec.sped.org/faq/gt-urls.htm

Gifted Resources Home Page
www.eskimo.com/~user/kids.html

Chapter VIII

Students with Communication Disorders

Definition

Communication disorders are disturbances in normal speech and language that disrupt the communication process sufficiently to interfere with the transference of ideas. Communication disorders may be speech disorders, which are problems in creating speech orally, or language disorders, which are problems in receiving, understanding or formulating ideas and information.

Types of communication disorders:

I. *Language learning disabilities* – impairments in language comprehension and/or other language symbol systems

   A. Impaired comprehension of forms of language

      1. *phonology* – the sequence of sounds in a word—incorrect sequence (fatser-faster) or the wrong sound (falser-faster)

      2. *morphology* – the combination of sounds to form meaningful units (boy + s = boys)

      3. *syntax* – the order of words in sentences (I store will to go the. I will go to the store.)

   B. *Impaired comprehension of language content (semantics)* – the substance, meaning, and relationship between words to determine meaning of a phrase or sentence (You can bank on my bank shot.)

   C. *Impaired comprehension of language function (pragmatics)* – communication in the social context, i.e., eye contact, body language, taking turns speaking, using vocabulary appropriate to the occasion

II. *Speech disorders* – difficulties performing the neuromuscular movements of speech, most commonly articulation disorders

   A. *Substitutions* – "th" for "s," "f" for" th," "w" for "r" (He lost his fwont toof.)

   B. *Omissions* – sounds left out of words (Gi' me a han'.)

   C. *Additions* – extra sounds added to words (Stop pushering me.)

III. *Fluency disorders* – irregularities which interfere with the normal flow of speech

A. *Stuttering* – an unwanted repetition of a sound within a word (G-g-g-get me out of he-e-e-ar.)

B. *Stammering* – long pauses between words, sometimes filled with repeated use of one of the words in the sentence or a meaningless sound (And, and, and, and, then we uh, uh, uh, urr, went to bed.)

IV. *Voice disorders* – qualities which make the speaker unpleasant to listen to

A. *Disorders of volume* – vocal quality is either too loud or too soft

B. *Disorders of pitch* – vocal quality is too high or too low

C. *Disorders of quality* – vocal quality is nasal, breathy, whining, shrill, etc.

V. *Variations in language models* – (not a disorder) any accent or dialect which deviates from Standard American English in vocabulary (I'm hangin' with my homey), pronunciation (Vat you vant frum me?), sentence structure (You want I too should go?), or use of individual words (This band is really "bad".) Ebonics, the variation of English often used by working class African-Americans, is the most discussed variation.

VI. Late talking and language delay

A. *Late talking* – lack of speech or inappropriate speech for age level with adequate comprehension. Children with language delay are also able to engage in pretending play with their peers.

B. *Language delay* – a lagging ability to communicate in speech and comprehension, usually accompanied by difficult-to-interpret gestures.

Important Facts about
Students with Communication Disorders

- The ability to communicate effectively is probably the most important skill human beings learn.

- Most children with language disorders continue to be taught in the regular classroom with resource services provided on a pull-out basis with a speech therapist.

- Students who have difficulty expressing themselves because of a communication disorder will have some days in which they can express themselves better than they can on other days.

- The cause of stuttering is unknown. Though recent theories blamed anxiety for stuttering, it is now felt that stuttering is a cause of anxiety.

- A student who chooses not to speak to a particular person or persons but understands what they are saying does not have a communication problem but an emotional problem called "elective muteness."

Characteristic Behavior of Students with Communication Disorders

- Display unpleasant vocal characteristics (e.g., too loud, too soft, too high, too nasal).

- Use extensive gestures and hand signals to replace words.

- Use vocabulary that is less than age appropriate.

- Exhibit a pronounced variation in speech.

- Omit the first or last sounds of words.

- Continue to mispronounce words after having been corrected.

- Often confuse pronouns.

- Have difficulty forming sentences.

- Omit words from sentences.

- Incorrectly sequence words within a sentence.

- Display an unnatural flow of words with extensive pauses.

- Exhibit similar difficulties in reading and writing.

- Misunderstand directions and may not ask for clarification.

- Are often misunderstood by teachers and other students.

- Seldom speak in class.

Suggestions for Working with a Student with Communication Disorders

- Be patient.

- Be accepting.

- Tell the student you understand his problem.

- Do not allow a student with a speech problem to be teased by other students; maintain a safe environment for all students to work on their skills.

- Model good English usage. Avoid using slang.

- Work with all students on building vocabulary. If you use a vocabulary workbook reinforce the words of the lessons in other subjects and in general classroom conversation. Do not feel reluctant to use new words even if they seem difficult. Children, especially the very young, have a great capacity for learning new words.

- Enunciate so the children can hear words pronounced correctly.

- Do not call attention to a speech problem in front of the class.

- If you feel a speech problem can be corrected with a minimal amount of work with the student, keep the student back briefly from recess or lunch to work on it.

- If you feel a student has made a mistake due to faulty learning, it is all right to correct the speaker.

- If a student speaks incorrectly, repeat the phrase correctly (e.g., If the student says, "I want to go 'fatser,' " respond, "You want to go 'faster?' ")

- Do not interrupt or finish words or sentences for students who have difficulty speaking.

- Do not imitate a student to show her how she sounds.

- Do not tape-record a student without his or her permission.

- Encourage poor speakers to talk. Set up situations where they have to speak to you; give them too few supplies so they have to ask for more; or put their boots on the wrong feet so they have to correct you. Engage them in conversations as much as you can.

- Help the students have conversations with each other by having them work in groups of threes or fours.

- Have the class occasionally do choral reading.

- Plan exercises in which the students make prepared speeches, even as short as a minute, in front of the class. If the student is uncomfortable giving a speech, do not insist it be given.

- Do not force students to read aloud or recite in front of the class if they strongly resist.

- Do not make a student more uncomfortable about having to speak in front of others.

- Ask if the student would like to be called on in class. Encourage a positive response but do not demand one.

- If a student has a volume or pitch problem ask her if changing the speech problem is desirable. If so, practice correct speech with the student. Develop a signal to alert the student to subsequent occurrences of the undesirable speech pattern.

- Ask students who speak with accents, or use Ebonics or heavy slang if they would prefer to speak mainstream English in school. If so, work with them to achieve that goal.

- Do not consider that other languages are inferior to Standard English and should be avoided at all times.

- Do not make negative comments about another language or language variation used outside of class.

- Do not demand that a student stop speaking another language.

- Do not show disrespect for the way a student speaks.

- Do not tell a student who stutters to stop stuttering, to slow down and think, or to take a deep breath before answering. Do not ask the student to start over if it is difficult to speak. Do not finish the word or sentence for the student. Do not appear angry, frustrated or impatient while the student is trying to speak. Do not threaten to punish the student for stuttering. The student is well aware of the problem without the teacher drawing attention to it.

- If a student with a stutter or other speech problem is having a good day with his speech, call on him as often as you can.

Glossary

aphasia – partial or total loss of speech

articulation – the ability to produce sounds

cleft palate – a split in the upper part of the oral cavity which causes a nasality in speaking

dialect – a regional or cultural variation of a language

Ebonics – a variation of Standard English most often spoken in working class African-American communities

fluency – the quality of speaking with normal rhythms, patterns and speed

grammar – the study of the placement of words in sentences

morpheme – the smallest meaningful unit of speech

morphology – the rules which dictate how morphemes will be used to form words

pitch – the quality of lowness or highness in the voice

phonemes – the different sounds in a language

phonology – the rules which dictate how a language is used in interactions between people

resonance – the quality of the voice

semantics – the rules which dictate how words are used meaningfully

syntax – the rules which dictate the order of words in a sentence

volume – the quality of loudness in the voice

Reference Books

Adler, S. *Oral Communication Problems in Children and Adolescents.* Philadelphia, PA: Crane and Stratton, 1998.

Costello, J., and A. Holland. *Handbook of Speech and Language Disorders.* San Diego, CA: College Hill Press, 1986.

Hedge, M.N. *Introduction to Communication Disorders.* Austin, TX: 1991.

Warren, S.F. *Enhancing Children's Communication.* Baltimore, MD: Paul H. Brookes, 1993.

Web Sites

American Speech–Language–Hearing Association
    www.asha.org

Center for Communitive and Congenitive Disabilities
    www.uwo.ca/cccd

Stuttering Foundation of America
    www.stutterSFA.org

The Unicorn Children's Foundation
    www.saveachild.com

Chapter IX

Students with Partial Hearing Loss and Deafness

- *Students with Partial Hearing Loss*
- *Students with Deafness*

Definitions

Hearing impairment [partial hearing loss] is an impairment in hearing whether permanent of fluctuating, that adversely affects a child's educational performance but which is not included under the definition of deafness. —IDEA

Deafness is hearing impairment that is so severe that the child is impaired in processing linguistic information through hearing, with or without amplification, that adversely affects a child's educational performance. —IDEA

Important Facts about Students with Partial Hearing Loss and Deafness

- Many people with hearing loss object to the term "hearing impaired." They feel it implies something lacking or something wrong with them. They see themselves as a separate culture with its own language and prefer to use the terms "deaf" and "people with hearing loss."

- Some of the diseases which can cause hearing loss and deafness are Otitis Media (middle ear infection), rubella, meningitis, prematurity, mother-child RH incompatibility, cytomegalovirus (CMV), and hereditary and genetic factors.

- About 30 percent of children with hearing loss also have another disability.

- In the past the average age of diagnosing a child with congenital hearing loss was 30 months, resulting in a long delay in teaching language skills. Current devices now test for hearing loss a few days after birth, providing the opportunity for language skills to be taught at an earlier age.

- Children with sensorineural hearing loss can have partial hearing restored with a cochlear implant. This procedure, still in its early stages, produces varying degrees of success. The deaf community does not support the procedure because they feel the deaf culture is a rich culture which people do not have to leave by way of a surgical procedure.

- Hearing loss alone has no effect on intelligence.

- In working with students with hearing loss the primary concern is to teach communication skills. Deaf students have a difficult time learning the spoken language. Therefore, they are often behind in reading skills and other academics where reading is required.

- About 90 percent of deaf children have hearing parents.

- Some parents of children with hearing loss never learn to communicate manually with their children.

Characteristic Behavior of
Students with Partial Hearing Loss and Deafness

- Routinely lag behind hearing students with similar intelligence in attaining communication skills. (This is particularly true among those with prelingual hearing loss.)

- May develop psychological problems because their hearing parents may have difficulty bonding with a deaf child.

- May have problems adjusting to a hearing society.

Characteristic Behavior of
Students with Undiagnosed Hearing Loss

- Have limited vocabulary.

- Lack proper speech development.

- Speak unclearly.

- Speak with unusual intonation.

- Stare at people's lips when they are speaking.

- Cock head or turn head to one side when listening.

- Ask classmates to repeat instructions just given.

- Ask a lot of questions about material or directions just given.

- Withdraw from oral activities.

- Work best in small groups.

- Engage in either acting-out or withdrawn behavior.

Students with Partial Hearing Loss

Suggestions for Working with a Student with Partial Hearing Loss

- Seat the student in the front of the room. If the student has unilateral hearing loss assign a seat so the student's better ear is nearer to you.

- If the student uses a hearing aid make sure it is in working order. Ask the parents for a supply of extra batteries.

- Try to get carpeting or rugs to improve the acoustics.

- Cut down on background noise by keeping windows closed in noisy neighborhoods and air conditioners low during oral presentations.

- If available, equip the student's desk with small speakers and wear a lapel microphone.

- Use visual aids whenever possible.

- Write important notes on the chalkboard.

- Allow the student to tape-record the lectures and class discussions.

- Assign student helpers to assist the student with taking notes and completing other activities that would clarify the classwork.

- Speak within 10 feet of a student who is wearing a hearing aid.

- Face the class when speaking so the student can watch your lips. Be careful not to speak while writing on the chalkboard.

- Do not hold objects or your hands in front of your mouth when talking.

- If you have a large moustache consider a shave or trim so your lips can be seen.

- Enunciate clearly.

- If the student is having trouble understanding you try rephrasing and slowing down. To ensure the student's correct understanding request that your instructions be repeated.

- Encourage the student to speak. If possible help develop proper pronunciation.

88

- Include the student in choral readings and class skits.
- Look for deficits in the student's social skills and provide training.

Students with Deafness

Suggestions for Working with a Student with Deafness

- Seat the student in the front of the room so he can see you speaking.
- During class discussions have the student who is talking stand so the deaf student can watch the speaker's lips.
- Assign a classmate each day to be the student's study-buddy. This person would help the student understand what is happening in the room, assist with note taking, and inform the student of any need to move from one place to another.
- Learn a few basic phrases in sign language and have the student teach them to the entire class.
- Give the student an advance copy of each day's agenda.
- Give the student an outline of the lessons.
- Review the vocabulary for the lesson and give the student an advance copy.
- Do not assume the student does not want to go to music class. If possible give the student the choice of going or doing something else.
- Encourage the use of computers and educational computer programs so the student can get additional learning without having to listen. Teach keyboard skills.
- Use videotapes and slides that have printed captions.
- Encourage the student to speak, unless you have been instructed not to by the parents or a school administrator.
- Tell the student how speech sounds. Make comments about pitch, speed, volume, intonation, pronunciation, etc.
- Do not be embarrassed when using words like "listen" or "hear."
- If it would be helpful, recommend speech therapy.
- Work closely with the parents to make sure they are reinforcing at home what is being taught in school.

Suggestions for Working with a Sign Language Interpreter

• Keep in mind that you are in charge of the learning. Before the sign language interpreter begins working in your classroom discuss room procedures which will be changed by the presence of an additional adult.

• At the end of each day discuss with the interpreter the next day's lessons. Make sure the interpreter understands the concepts which are to be taught.

• Because the student may have difficulty watching your demonstration and the interpreter's signing at the same time, position yourselves so the student can view you both simultaneously.

• When speaking to the student do not look at the interpreter. Look at the student as in any other conversation. The interpreter will encode the message so the student can understand it. Allow the interpreter enough time to do this.

• It is all right for the sign language interpreter to work with other students if the primary responsibility remains with the student with hearing loss.

• Give rest periods to the speech language interpreter.

Glossary

acquired hearing loss – hearing loss that occurs to a person born with hearing

audiogram – a graph which displays the results of a hearing test

audiologist – a specialist trained to diagnose hearing disorders

aural habilitation – the practice of having students with hearing loss work with their residual hearing

bilateral hearing loss – hearing loss in both ears

conductive hearing loss – damage in the middle ear which causes some hearing loss but can be treated medically

congenital hearing loss – hearing loss that happens at birth

cochlear implant – a surgically implanted device which converts sound into electrical impulses stimulating the auditory nerve fibers to allow hearing

deaf culture / deaf community – a unique culture of people with hearing loss who communicate through manual language

decibel – a unit of loudness

hard of hearing – having some hearing loss but able to hear with amplification

mixed hearing loss – a combination of conductive and sensorineural hearing loss

postlingual hearing loss – hearing loss that happens after a child learns to speak

prelingual hearing loss – hearing loss that happens before a child learns to speak

residual hearing – the hearing that remains

sensorineural hearing loss – damage to the sensory nerve in the inner ear which usually results in irreversible and permanent hearing loss

unilateral hearing loss – hearing loss in only one ear

Methods of Communication Used by the Deaf

American Sign Language (ASL) – a visual gestural language indigenous to the American Deaf community, which is not sign code for English but a unique language with its own syntax and grammar (often acquired as a first language by deaf children who have deaf parents)

cued speech – a language method which uses coded hand shapes on the side of the face to supplement the sounds used in speech

fingerspell – a manual code technique with a configuration for each letter of the alphabet allowing words to be spelled letter by letter (good for conveying proper nouns but slow when used to convey entire thoughts)

manually coded English (MCE) – a visual manually spoken code with several variations which represents English (preferred by many teachers because its close relationship to English makes it easier for students to learn English)

Pidgin Sign English (PSE) – varieties of signing used by deaf and hearing people which combine elements of ASL and English

oral / aural method – a communication technique that stresses the use of speech, hearing aids, voice, and speech reading skills to help children function in a speaking society

Linguistics of Visual English (LOVE) – a manual technique with a unique configuration for each English syllable allowing words to be signed one syllable at a time

signed English – a system that uses ASL signs in English word order

The Rochester Method – a technique that uses fingerspell as words are simultaneously spoken

speech reading – the technique of watching lip movements and body language to gain meaning

total communication – the technique of speaking and signing simultaneously

Reference Books

Bowe, Frank. *Changing the Rules.* Silver Spring, MD: T.J. Publishers, 1986.

Mindel, Eugene D., and Vernon McCray, eds. *They Grow in Silence: Understanding Deaf Children and Adults.* San Diego, CA: College-Hill, 1987.

Moores, D.F. *Educating the Deaf: Psychology, Principals and Practices.* 4th ed. Boston, MA: Houghton Mifflin, 1996.

Schirmer, B.R. *Language and Literacy Development in Children Who Are Deaf.* Needham Heights, MA: Allyn & Bacon, 1994.

Schwartz, S. *Choices in Deafness: A Parent's Guide.* Rockville, MD: Woodbine House, 1987.

Web Sites

American Speech–Language–Hearing Association (ASHA)
www.asha.org

Council on Education of the Deaf
www.educ.kent.edu/deafed

Deaf World Web
  www.deafworldweb.org

Gallaudet University
  www.gallaudet.edu

National Institute on Deafness and Other Communication Disorders
  www.nih.gov/nidcd

Chapter X

Students with Low Vision and Blindness

- *Students with Low Vision*
- *Students with Blindness*

Definition

Visually handicapped means a visual impairment that, even with correction, adversely affects a child's educational performance.

—IDEA

Important Facts about
Students with Low Vision and Blindness

- Normal vision is 20/20 and a normal visual field is 160 degrees.

- Many people who are legally blind have some residual vision.

- Blind people do not develop better hearing. They simply learn to use their hearing to better advantage.

- Many blind people do not read braille or do not read it fluently. Blind people are more dependent on hearing written material read to them.

- The most important things a blind person must learn are orientation, mobility and independent living.

- Blindness has no relation to intelligence. The scholastic expectations of a blind student should be the same as those of a sighted student. However, the amount of work produced may differ.

- There are a number of technological advances, many quite expensive, that have been made to help the blind have better orientation, mobility and instruction in school.

- Schools may be reluctant to purchase many of the devices to aid vision because of their high cost.

- Sighted children can visualize a whole learning activity and then seek to understand each part. Blind children must learn the parts and then develop an understanding of the whole.

- Blind children cannot determine cause and effect as easily as sighted children because they cannot observe the result of an action.

- Blind children do not have equal opportunity for incidental learning because they cannot observe the activity going on around them.

- Blind children do not have equal opportunity to learn vocabulary because early vocabulary is built on naming familiar objects.

- Blind children have difficulty learning behavioral nuances necessary for successful socialization.

- Blind children are not able to participate in some early skill-building activities.

- Students with acquired blindness (those who were born with eyesight but have lost it) may harbor anger over their situation. They make take it out on the teacher by saying things such as "How would you like to be blind?"

- Blind students are accustomed to terms such as "look here" or "see what I mean" and are not offended by them.

- Parents of blind children sometimes have difficulty bonding with their children because a blind child does not gaze into their eyes. They may not play as long with a blind child as with a sighted child.

- Most schools provide students with a yearly vision screening which merely alerts parents of a vision problem that should be looked into. The students are usually given a notice to take home to their parents, which means the parents may or may not get it.

- Guide dogs are not pets. They are allowed in school as well as all public places, including restaurants. They are working dogs and are not in class for the other children to play with. Permission should be sought before petting or interacting with a guide dog.

- If people wish to take a blind student by the arm in order to serve as a guide, they should ask permission from the blind person first. While moving with a blind person it is helpful to describe where you are going and what you are passing.

- People who are legally blind are entitled to certain benefits such as an extra tax deduction on their income tax.

Students with Low Vision

Definition

Low vision is a condition in which a person can read only with the assistance of magnifying aids and/or large print.

Characteristic Behavior of Students with Low Vision

- Display uneven abilities in different areas.
- See and work better on some days than others.
- Adapt well socially and educationally.
- Capable of adhering to class standards of discipline and behavior.

Characteristic Behavior of Students with Undiagnosed Vision Problems

- Squint, blink and constantly rub eyes.
- Strain to see the chalkboard.
- Lack coordinated eye movement.
- Are oversensitive to light.
- Have eyes that itch, burn, water or tear.
- Have headaches.
- Feel nauseous.
- Hold books too close or too far away from the face.
- Move books in closer and farther from face while reading.
- Shut or cover one eye while reading.
- Read for a brief period and then put the reading material down.
- Tend to lose place when reading.
- Confuse similar looking letters.
- Guess at words when reading.
- Align writing poorly.

Suggestions for Working with a Student with Low Vision

- Seat the student near windows at the front of the room to provide natural light and avoid the glare of the sun.
- Allow the student to choose seats for different activities if it will help the student to see better.

- For greater contrast and readability use an overhead projector rather than writing on the chalkboard.

- Keep a large magnifying glass available.

- Acquire a set of large print textbooks, workbooks and reading materials.

- Talk to the parents and the special education teacher about the availability of vision aids for the classroom. Become an advocate for the student to help obtain whatever devices are necessary.

- Provide the student with pencils that have soft dark lead.

- If the student often forgets his eyeglasses at home, arrange with the parents to have an extra pair kept in school.

- Look for alternatives to games in which a small ball must be hit or caught.

- Allow the student to get help from other students when reading becomes tiring.

- Provide the student with lesson plans or outlines in advance to make it easier to follow your lessons.

- Allow the student to tape-record lessons to play at home.

- Allow the student extra time to do classwork.

- Allow the student to complete written assignments by speaking into a tape recorder.

- Modify homework assignments by omitting easy work and reducing the number of problems that must be completed.

- Help the student develop social skills.

Students with Blindness

Definitions

Functionally blind describes a person who has some residual vision, which is insufficient to read print, and must rely on other senses to perform daily living activities

Legally blind is a legal term which describes an ability of less than 20/200 in the better eye with correction or a field of vision less than 20 degrees.

Totally blind describes a person who has no vision and is totally dependent on other senses to perform daily living activities.

In this text the term "blindness" includes functionally blind, legally blind and totally blind.

Characteristic Behavior of Students with Blindness

There can be a wide range of behaviors for people with blindness which are largely determined by the time of the onset of their blindness. Children who became blind will have certain knowledge and skills that children who were born blind will not have.

- May perform self-stimulating behaviors such as hitting their head and face, scratching their eyes, rocking, etc.

- Prone to accidents and injury.

- Adjust well in most classes.

- Will have vocabulary deficits.

- May have social deficits.

Suggestions for Working with a Student with Blindness

- Request braille copies of workbooks and textbooks.

- Permit the student to explore the classroom and school.

- Provide the student with extra storage space if necessary.

- Though there is a tendency to be overprotective of a blind student, allow the student to take some risks.

- Give the student a normal amount of praise. Do not be excessive.

- If the student has an outburst of anger due to acquired blindness, do not be offended. Assure the student that you are available to help with the work for the entire school year.

- Try to eliminate self-stimulating behaviors.

- Develop daily-living skills.

- Plan activities to help the student develop social skills.

- Develop organizational skills.

- Develop communication skills.

- Help the student to learn to listen critically.

- Use tactile objects in as many lessons as possible.

- In geography try to provide the student with relief maps.

- In art encourage the student to work with varied materials.

- In math allow the student to do only the number of problems necessary to gain the skill.

- In math allow the student to use a talking calculator.

- In PE encourage exercises and activities which promote increased strength and body coordination.

- Encourage participation in music and drama.

- Allow lessons to be tape-recorded for review at home.

- Allow the student to speak into a tape recorder to complete written assignments.

- Be clear and specific when giving instructions.

- Allow extra time to complete assignments.

- Allow the student to skip over easy parts of the assignment.

- Involve the entire class. Use study-buddies to help the student with recording assignments, taking notes, moving from room to room, etc. When writing on the chalkboard have the buddy read what is being written.

- Include the student in all class activities.

- During class discussions have all the students begin speaking by identifying themselves.

- Teach the class not to move furniture or leave belongings lying around on the floor.

- Plan group activities which involve discussion and planning.

- Expect the same standards of behavior that you expect from all your students.

- Help the student meet other blind people in the community, especially successful blind people who could be good role models.

Glossary

acquired blindness – blindness which develops or occurs after birth

albinism – a hereditary condition characterized by lack of the pigment melanin causing a loss of visual acuity and extreme sensitivity to sunlight

astigmatism – a condition caused by an irregularly shaped cornea causing objects to look blurred

cataracts – a clouding of the lens in the eye causing unclear vision

color blindness – the inability to see some or all colors (more common in boys than in girls)

congenital blindness – blindness which has been present since birth

cross-eyed – a condition in which the pupils both go to the inner part of the cornea (see strabismus)

diabetic retinopathy – a condition in which poor blood circulation through the vessels in the retina causes damage and possible blindness

farsightedness – (see hyperopia)

glaucoma – a condition in which fluid collects inside the eye causing pressure and damage to the optic nerve

Hoover cane – the red and white cane used by the blind to aid in orientation and mobility

hyperopia (farsightedness) – a condition that blurs sight of near objects but retains clear vision of objects that are far away

macular degeneration – a condition in which the ability to see color and detail becomes impaired

myopia (nearsightedness) – a condition that blurs sight of far objects but retains clear vision of objects that are near

nearsightedness – (see myopia)

nystagmus – repetitive involuntary movement of the eye which causes lack of visual acuity

optic nerve atrophy – a disorder of the optic nerve which results in reduced visual acuity or low vision *optic nerve hypoplasia* – a disorder of the optic nerve that will result in a visual impairment or blindness

retinitis pigmentosa – a progressive eye disease caused by a deposit of pigmentation on the back of the retina resulting in a small field of vision

retinopathy of prematurity – damage to the retina, which may lead to blindness, caused by excessive oxygen given to premature babies

Snellen Chart – the chart used in a doctor's office to test visual acuity

strabismus – a problem with the eye muscles causing a person to appear cross-eyed or wall-eyed and possibly leading to reduced or lost vision in the weaker eye

tunnel vision – a condition which allows the viewer to see only a small area at a time

visual acuity – the measure of how well a person can see

wall-eyed – a condition in which one or both eyes involuntarily go to the outer sides of the cornea (see strabismus)

Reference Books

Olmstead, Jean E. *Itinerant Teaching: Tricks of the Trade for Teachers of Blind and Visually Impaired Students.* New York, NY: American Foundation for the Blind, 1991.

Rug, Sally M. *Helping the Visually Impaired Child with Developmental Problems: Effective Practice in Home, School, and Community.* New York, NY: Teachers College Press, 1988.

Scholl, Geraldine T. *Foundations of Education for Blind and Visually Handicaped Children and Youth: Theory and Practice.* New York, NY: American Foundation for the Blind, 1986.

Web Sites

American Foundation for the Blind
www.afb.org/afb

American Printing House for the Blind
www.aph.org

Resources for Parents and Teachers of Blind Kids
www.az.com/~dday/blindkids.html

Chapter XI

Students with Traumatic Brain Injury

Definition

Traumatic brain injury is an acquired injury to the brain caused by an external physical force, resulting in total or partial functional disability or psychosocial impairment, or both, that adversely affects a child's educational performance. The term applies to open or closed head injuries resulting in impairments in one or more areas, such as cognition; language; memory; attention; reasoning; abstract thinking; judgment; problem-solving; sensory, perceptual, and motor abilities; psychosocial behavior; physical functions; information processing; and speech. The term does not apply to brain injuries that are congenital or degenerative, or brain injuries induced by birth trauma.

—IDEA

Important Facts about Students with Traumatic Brain Injury

- The three main causes of traumatic brain injury are automobile accidents, sports and recreational accidents, and violence.

- Students may have undiagnosed closed-head traumatic brain injury, particularly shaken-impact or shaken-baby syndrome, due to child abuse.

- All cases of traumatic brain injury have their own manifestations. Every case is different.

- Thirty years ago 90 percent of people who suffered brain injuries died. Due to advances in science and medicine, the figure today is 50 percent. Consequently, the classroom teacher can expect to encounter more students with traumatic brain injury.

- Although the student may recover from traumatic brain injury, it is likely the incident will cause some permanent changes in behavior.

- The effects of traumatic brain injury change as the brain repairs itself or learns to redirect its functioning. Many are not noticeable immediately. Some may appear days or weeks later. Therefore, the student's abilities should be reassessed frequently.

- In addition to coping with skills lost, the student must also cope with a slowed process of learning new skills.

- Children who suffer from traumatic brain injury understand their problem. They are often angry and frustrated because they can no longer perform certain tasks with the skill they once had.

- While recovering from an accident involving traumatic brain injury, the student may receive some schooling in the hospital or at home. However, the student should be encouraged to return to school as soon as possible.

Characteristic Behavior of
Students with Traumatic Brain Injury

Physical behaviors

- Have lost skills in some areas but not in others. (This is particularly true in open head wounds where only the areas of the brain touched by the wound are affected.)

- Have epileptic seizures.

- Show signs of paralysis or spasticity.

- Exhibit coordination problems.

- React adversely to touch or smell.

- Exhibit weakness, fatigue or problems with sleep.

- Have frequent headaches.

- Develop vision or hearing problems.

Cognitive behaviors

- Have difficulty concentrating or paying attention.

- Have problems with both long and short term memory.

- Have difficulty solving problems and reasoning.

- Think more slowly.

- Have difficulty planning and sequencing.

- Demonstrate poor judgment and lack of insight.

- Exhibit loss of some academic abilities.

Linguistic behaviors

- Unable to speak for a period of time (aphasia). (Expressive language is usually recovered as the wound heals.)

- Revert to immature language.

- Have problems understanding language.

- Speak slowly.

- Have difficulty finding the right word.

- Have difficulty following instructions.

Psychological behaviors

- Exhibit personality changes.

- Have difficulty with self-identity.

- Exhibit increased egocentrism.

- Respond with increased or decreased emotion.

- Are depressed, irritable or anxious.

- Exhibit poor coping abilities and reduced social skills.

- Are fearful of new situations.

Suggestions for Working with a
Student with Traumatic Brain Injury

- Revolve the student's education around a four point program: (1) recover old skills, (2) develop new skills, (3) compensate for unrecoverable skills, and (4) adjust to personality changes.

- Because of changes in abilities due to healing, review and revise the IEP every few weeks.

- Keep good records of what the student is learning and not learning.

- Try to reinforce the work being done by the ancillary staff (speech therapist, occupational therapist, physical therapist, social worker, tutor, etc.) who are working with the student.

- Capitalize on retained abilities and skills.

- Develop rewards programs to encourage positive changes in behavior.

- Help the rest of the class to understand the nature of the student's changes in behavior and encourage them to remain friends.

- Assign a classmate to help the student understand all his assignments and, if necessary, give help throughout the day's activities.

- Define words or use synonyms if the student does not understand what is being said.

- Provide the student with both verbal and written instructions. Check for compliance.

- Repeat verbal instructions. Use different ways of saying what you want to express if the student does not seem to understand the instructions the first time.

- If the student is unable to contend with lengthy instructions, shorten instruction times and give the student opportunities to rest.

- Allow the student to rest and temporarily stop working.

- Modify classwork and homework expectations.

- Structure lessons to include several small group discussions.

- Allow the student extra time to finish the work.

- Allow the student to tape-record lessons in class.

- Assist the student in keeping his desk, work and books neat and orderly.

- Do not let the student guess at answers. Tell the student the answer instead and work with the student to reinforce remembering it.

- Use repetition.

- Insist on appropriate work and appropriate classroom behavior.

To improve attention

- Remove distractions, such as books and supplies, not necessary for the immediate work.

- Limit the amount of information given at one time.

- Adjust the assignments to be compatible with the student's attention span.

- Bring the student into focus with statements calling attention to what you are about to do.

To improve language comprehension and the ability to follow directions

- Limit the amount of directives to one or two at a time.

- Use language that is concrete.

- Tell the student to ask for more information if he doesn't understand what to do.

- Use examples and pictures to help the student to understand.

- Use gestures and body language to help clarify directions.

To improve memory

- Have a classmate help the student take notes. Allow the lessons to be tape-recorded.

- Have the student keep a journal of the day's activities and assignments.

- Highlight key information in the readings.

- Provide the student with a schedule of the day's activities.

- Have the student repeat important information back to you. Allow the student to practice repeating key information.

- Provide the student with pictures and other visual cues.

- Practice rote memorization.

To improve sequencing

- Break each task into short steps. List and number each step. Assign the steps to the student one or two at a time.

- Give cues to the student to remember the next step.

- Remind the student of how many steps are necessary and how many are already completed.

- Provide written directions or diagrams which will cue the next step.

To improve thought organization

- Teach the student to place thoughts into categories.

- Focus on one type of information at a time.

- Encourage the student to try to organize slowly and thoroughly before beginning a procedure.

To improve generalization

- Provide the student with a format for solving problems. Help him to use the format in more than one situation.

- Provide the student with samples of work which were done correctly.

- Do similar work in two different ways, such as answering questions by filling in the blanks on a worksheet and then on a computer.

Glossary

acquired brain injury – any injury to the brain either traumatic or non-traumatic

aphasia – partial or total loss of speech

cognitive training – instruction to regain lost psychological processes

lobe – a section of the brain

non-traumatic brain injury – damage to the brain caused by toxins, infections, strokes, tumors and anoxic injuries (lack of oxygen)

shaken impact syndrome (shaken baby syndrome) – brain trauma inflicted at an early age by an adult violently shaking a child so that the head moves back and forth rapidly, causing the brain to be injured from hitting the inside of the skull

trauma – a physical or psychological blow

Reference Books

Gronwall, D. and P. Waddell. *Head Injury—The Facts.* Oxford University Press, 1998.

Stein, Donald G., Simon Brailowsky, and Bruno Will. *Brain Repair.* Oxford University Press, 1995.

Stoler, Diane Roberts, and Barbara Albers Hill. *Coping with Mild TBI.* New York, NY: Avery Hill Publishing Company, 1998.

Web Sites

Brain Injury Association
  www.biausa.org

The Brain Injury Connection
  www.tbihelp.com/BIC

National Institute on Disability and Rehabilitation Research -
  Traumatic Brain Injury
  www.tbims.org

Chapter XII

Students with Severe and Multiple Disabilities

- *Students with Severe and Profound Mental Retardation*
- *Students with Schizophrenia*
- *Students with Multiple Disabilities*

Definition

The term "children with severe disabilities" refers to children with disabilities who, because of the intensity of their physical, mental, or emotional problems, need highly specialized education, social, psychological, and medical services in order to maximize their full potential for useful and meaningful participation in society and for self-fulfillment. The term includes those children with disabilities with severe emotional disturbance (including schizophrenia), autism, severe and profound mental retardation, and those who have two or more serious disabilities such as deaf-blindness, mental retardation and blindness, and cerebral palsy and deafness. Children with severe disabilities may experience severe speech, language, and/or perceptual-cognitive deprivations and evidence abnormal behaviors such as failure to respond to pronounced social stimuli, self-mutilation, self-stimulation, manifestation of intense and prolonged temper tantrums, and the absence of rudimentary forms of verbal control; and may also have intensely fragile physiological conditions.

—IDEA

Important Facts about Students with Severe and Multiple Disabilities

- Many educators question the practice of including students with severe and multiple disabilities in the regular classroom because the student will not be able to do any of the work the rest of the class is doing.

- The value of having students with severe disabilities in the regular classroom is to give them an opportunity to interact with their peers and to give their peers an opportunity to interact with them.

Suggestions for Working with a Student with Severe and Multiple Disabilities

- If a student with severe or multiple disabilities is being placed in your classroom, attend the staffing and play an active role in forming the Individual Education Plan (IEP). If anything is presented that is beyond your capabilities or inappropriate for a classroom teacher attempt to work out an alternative plan.

- Accept a student with severe or multiple disabilities into your classroom only when the following questions have been answered satisfactorily:

  1. Why is this student being placed in my classroom? Is it to be with the appropriate age group or merely to satisfy the whims of his parents?

  2. What strengths does this student have? What capabilities?

  3. What are the goals for this student? Are they realistic and consistent with the abilities of the student or are they the product of denial and wishful thinking?

  4. What support services are being supplied for this student? Are they adequate for the student's needs?

  5. Will the student have a full-time aid? What happens on the days the aid is absent? Will the student also be kept at home or will the classroom teacher have to provide the care? If a substitute aid is called will it be someone with prior training?

  6. What specialized services will the regular classroom teacher be expected to provide for the student? Are these extra assignments reasonable to require? Will any of them be inappropriate, such as doing toileting or medical procedures?

  7. How will this student be graded?

- If you are being forced to take a student with inadequate and inappropriate support do not argue with the principal at the staffing, but notify the union as soon as possible. If the union cannot intervene or there is no union, accept the student and do the best job you can under the circumstances. Do not feel guilty or personally responsible for any shortfalls in the student's education. Instead, feel a sense of accomplishment for any gains made.

Students with Severe and Profound Mental Retardation

Definitions

Severe retardation is a condition in which a person has an I.Q. from 20 to 35 and requires extensive support and supervision.

Profound retardation is a condition in which a person has an I.Q. less than 20 and requires constant support and supervision.

The I.Q. ranges included in this section are meant to serve only as a reference and not as a solitary factor in determining the subcategories. There are other rating scales which evaluate the abilities of these students.

Important Facts about
Students with Severe and Profound Mental Retardation

- Severe and profound mental retardation may be associated with another disability, such as cerebral palsy.

- Students with severe and profound mental retardation respond positively to contact and acceptance from adults and peers.

- It is all right for the student's aid to work with other students in the class.

Suggestions for Working with a
Student with Severe and Profound Mental Retardation

- Welcome the student and the accompanying aid into the class and introduce them to the other students. Continue to treat the student like any other new student.

- Allow the student's classmates to ask questions about the student and the aid. Answer them as honestly as you can. Invite the student's parents to participate in this discussion.

- Encourage the class to work with the student by talking, reading, drawing, or eating with the student, pushing the student's wheelchair, or doing anything appropriate that would enrich both the disabled and the regular students.

- Encourage the parents of the student's classmates to invite the student to birthday parties and other out-of-school activities.

- If the student uses a communication board teach the student's classmates how to use it so they can talk to the student.

- Provide the student with a functional curriculum which stresses communication and self-care and encourages the participation of classmates in these areas.

- Provide opportunities for the student to learn socialization and home-living skills.

- If the student is capable give instructions about health, safety and the community.

- Include the student in as many activities as is possible.

- If the student must receive services outside the classroom, try to schedule these services so the student receives maximum participation in your classroom.

- Interact with the student beyond giving assignments to the aid. With the aid determine your role and the role of the aid.

Students with Schizophrenia

Definition

[Schizophrenia exhibits these] characteristic symptoms: Two (or more) of the following, each present for a significant portion of time during a 1-month period (or less if successfully treated): (1) delusions (2) hallucinations (3) disorganized speech (e.g. frequent derailment or incoherence) (4) grossly disorganized catatonic behavior (5) negative symptoms i.e. affective flattening, alogia or avolition...

—American Psychiatric Association

(Reprinted with permission from the *Diagnostic and Statistical Manual of Mental Disorders*, Fourth Edition. Copyright 1994 American Psychiatric Association.)

Important Facts about Students with Schizophrenia

- Contrary to popular opinion, schizophrenia does not mean split personality nor does it refer to people with more than one personality, such as Sybil or Eve who had multiple personality disorder. Rather, schizophrenia indicates a shattered personality.

- Schizophrenia has varying degrees of severity. Some students exhibit constant symptoms, while others have episodes that come and go.

- Some students with schizophrenia can control the effects with medication. Though the medication often produces side effects, such as drowsiness, decreased attention, and tremors, these side effects are preferable to a student having schizophrenic symptoms.

- The incidence of schizophrenia is low in the elementary grades but increases in junior and senior high school because puberty is the common time of onset.

- In some cases students with schizophrenia can cause harm to themselves and others.

- It is beneficial to have an aid in the classroom, although the aid need not be strictly for the student with schizophrenia.

- A student on medication may experiment to see what would happen if the medication is skipped. The results can be disastrous.

- Some students with schizophrenia learn to function in society by the time they reach adulthood. Others do not.

Characteristic Behavior of Students with Schizophrenia

- Neglect personal care.

- Lack friends.

- Withdraw to a point of not responding to anyone.

- Are depressed.

- Have extreme and sudden mood changes.

- Do schoolwork poorly.

- Exhibit emotions inappropriate to the situation.

- Act in a bizarre manner.

- Tell of personal experiences which are difficult to believe.

- Talk in an unusual and incomprehensible manner, often using unknown words.

- Interpret the environment and past events in an unusual manner.

- Exhibit obsessive behavior more severe than a student with obsessive/compulsive disorder.

- Have a vivid imagination (related to hallucinations and delusions).

- Talk to themselves.

- Are afraid for irrational reasons.

Suggestions for Working with a Student with Schizophrenia

- Focus on teaching in areas in which the student needs learning.

- Allow flexibility in complying with classroom activities.

- Establish a plan to accommodate the student if the student's behavior prevents participation in classroom activities.

- When the student is acting appropriately, include the student in as many classroom activities as possible.

- Inquire about the student's medication and its effects. Be prepared to accommodate the effects when they occur.

- If the student is taking medication make sure the medication has been taken.

- If an aid is already present in the room for another student discuss with the administration whether the aid can play a role in the education of the student with schizophrenia.

- If the student's condition could possibly threaten classroom safety devise a plan to protect the student, classmates, the aid and yourself if a dangerous situation should arise. If the student's condition continually threatens classroom safety, question the advisability of the inclusion placement.

Students with Multiple Disabilities

Definition

Multiple disabilities means concomitant impairments (such as mental retardation-blindness, mental retardation-orthopedic impairment, etc.), the combination of which causes such severe educational problems that they cannot be accommodated in special education programs solely for one of the impairments. The term does not include deaf-blindness. —IDEA

Important Facts about Students with Multiple Disabilities

- Accidents and some disorders, such as cerebral palsy, phenylketonuria (PKU), encephalocele, and amniotic band syndrome, are the most common causes of multiple disabilities.

- Most students with multiple disabilities have severe impairments in intellectual functioning.

- Most of the students will have limited communication abilities.

- Hearing and vision are likely to be affected.

- If the student is in a wheelchair or other supportive device, it is important that the student get out of the device several times a day and exercise gross muscles.

- During the school day many students with multiple disabilities need health care related to breathing, digestion, and elimination processes. This is the responsibility of the aid or school nurse. The classroom teacher should not be expected to fill this role. However, the classroom teacher may volunteer to do so.

- Students with multiple disabilities respond positively to warmth and human contact.

Suggestions for Working with a Student with Multiple Disabilities

- Discuss with your class the student with multiple disabilities. Answer all questions as honestly as possible. Encourage the parents of the student to participate in this discussion.

- Introduce the student to the class as you would any other new student. Encourage the classmates to introduce themselves.

- Interact with the student in more ways than merely giving the student's assignments to the aid.

- Determine and develop the student's strengths.

- Emphasize communication skills.

- If the student has a communication board teach the student how to use it effectively and allow the student's classmates to use it to communicate with the student.

- If possible teach self-care skills.

- Include the student in as many classroom activities as possible.

- Encourage the class to interact with the student on a daily basis. Each day assign one class member to push the student's wheelchair and do other helpful chores.

- Encourage the student to feed himself, even if it takes a long time and is messy.

- Enact a plan with the aid to make the aid's presence beneficial to the entire class.

- If the student is in a wheelchair make sure that correct posture is maintained at all times and that the seat belt is secured when the chair is moving.

- Allow the student to move about the room if necessary.

Glossary

affective flattening – restriction in the range of emotional expression

alogia – inability to speak because of a mental difficulty or an episode of dementia

augmentative communication – communication other than reading, writing, and speaking

avolition –inability to initiate goal-directed behavior

catatonic – a type of behavior characterized by mental stupor and a rigid body which appears to be frozen in position, alternating with periods of extreme excitement

childhood psychosis – (see pervasive developmental disorder)

clean intermittent catheterization (CIC) – the insertion of a catheter into the urethra to drain urine

delusion – a mistake in thinking which results in an incorrect interpretation of the events taking place

echolalia – the parroting of words or phrases usually immediately after they are heard

encephalocele – a disorder in which the skull does not close but develops a membrane to cover the brain tissue

encopresis/enuresis – incontinence of feces and urine (often a symptom of a severe disability)

facilitated communication – a procedure using a communication board which enables many with limited or no communication ability to have some communication (the degree of success will vary with the individual)

functional curriculum – a curriculum which focuses on developing skills in communication, self care, home living, community living, socialization, and job skills

gastrostomy – tube feeding; feeding directly into the intestine through a tube

hallucination – a sensory misinterpretation of an experience

mania – excessive excitement usually centered on a specific object or event

neologism – a word coined by a person with schizophrenia which has no meaning to other people

neuroleptics – anti-psychotic drugs which suppress the symptoms of schizophrenia

pervasive developmental disorder – a distortion or lag in all or several areas of personal development

psychotic disorder – an emotional disorder or behavioral disorder characterized by bizarre thinking, feeling and acting

respiratory ventilation – a procedure for suctioning off mucus through a small tube

stereotypical behavior – persistent repetition of an action or speech pattern

Reference Books

Children with Disabilities. 4th ed. Edited by Mark L. Bradshaw. Baltimore, MD: Paul H. Brookes, 1997.

Ferguson, Dianne and Searl, Stanford J., Jr. *The Challenge of Integrating Students with Severe Disabilities.* Syracuse, N.Y: Syracuse University Press.

Orelove, F., and D. Sobsey. *Educating Children with Multiple Disabilities.* Baltimore, MD: Paul H. Brookes, 1991.

Thompson, Barbara. *A Circle of Inclusion: Facilitating the Inclusion of Young Children with Severe Disabilities in Mainstream Early Childhood Educational Programs.* Lawrence, KS: University of Kansas Press, 1993.

Web Sites

Facts for Families
  www.aacap.org/factsfam

Mental Retardation Research Center
  www.mrrc.npi.ucla.edu

Chapter XIII

Students with Physical Disabilities

- *Students with Neurological Conditions*
  - *Students with Cerebral Palsy and Spina Bifida*
  - *Students with Epilepsy*

- *Students with Musculoskeletal Conditions*
  - *Students with Juvenile Rheumatoid Arthritis*
  - *Students with Muscular Dystrophy*

- *Students with Spinal Cord Injuries*

Definition

"Physical disability" or "orthopedic impairment" means a severe orthopedic impairment that adversely affects a child's educational performance. The term includes impairment caused by a congenital anomaly (club foot, missing limb), impairments caused by disease (polio), and impairments from other causes, (cerebral palsy, amputation, fracture, burns that cause contractures).

—IDEA

(Traumatic brain injury is covered in Chapter XI – Students with Traumatic Brain Injury.)

Important Facts about Students with Physical Disabilities

- A physical disability is a condition that incapacitates to some degree the skeletal and/or neuromuscular systems of the body.

- A physical disability may not affect the intellectual power of the student. If only bodily function is impaired, the problems can be compensated.

- A student with a physical disability should be treated as an integral part of the class, not just a person sharing the room. The teacher must model this behavior so the class can understand it.

- Students with physical disabilities are subject to teasing and physical abuse.

- If the student has an aid: *(a)* the teacher, not the aid, should be in charge of the student's education; *(b)* the teacher and the aid should determine what the aid's role will be in the room and with the other students; and *(c)* the teacher and the aid should be as flexible and creative as they like.

Suggestions for Working with a Student with Physical Disabilities

- If a student with a physical disability is becoming one of your students, talk to the class about the new student. The school nurse, the student's parents and the student may wish to join the discussion. Encourage the class to ask questions. Answer them honestly and in understandable terms.

- Before the student enters the class, inform the class that the student with a physical disability is a fellow student for whom everyone is responsible. If appropriate assign tasks to different members of the class related to the care of the student, such as pushing the wheelchair, getting lunch, helping with books or a coat. Alternate helpers so that every member of the class has an opportunity to participate.

Students with Neurological Conditions

Students with Cerebral Palsy and Spina Bifida

Definitions

Cerebral palsy is an impairment of the communication process between the brain and the muscles caused by damage to the brain before or during birth or during infancy and resulting in four types of abnormal physical movement:

1. spasticity – mild to severe exaggeration of contractions of the muscles when they are stretching;

2. dyskenesia – involuntary extraneous motor activity, especially when under stress;

3. ataxia – a lurching walking gait; or

4. mixed types – a combination of the above.

Spina bifida is a congenital defect in which the spine has not closed correctly causing the spinal cord to protrude from the weak point.

Important Facts about Students with Cerebral Palsy

- Some students will need only slight modifications to classroom procedures, while others will need major adjustments.

- Many students will need additional services such as speech therapy, occupational therapy, physical therapy, and adaptive PE.

- Some students will also display mental retardation, hearing loss, hyperactivity, and visual impairments.

- All students will suffer a lack of muscle coordination.

Important Facts about Students with Spina Bifida

- The higher up the spinal cord the problem occurs, the more disabled the student will be.

- Other problems associated with spina bifida of which the teacher and aid should be aware are *(a)* increased temperature, *(b)* flushed skin, *(c)* excessive perspiration, *(d)* incontinence, and *(e)* injuries to the lower extremities of which the student may be unaware.

- Some children with spina bifida have hydrocephalus and may have to wear a shunt. If the student complains of a headache, has a seizure, becomes sleepy, or vomits, it may be an indication of shunt failure.

Suggestions for Working with a Student with Cerebral Palsy or Spina Bifida

- Give the student access to all parts of the room.

- Give the student ample opportunities to exercise.

- If the student's mental capacity has not been affected, provide the student with appropriate work.

- Make sure the student is comfortable in the wheelchair.

- Make provisions for the student to get out of the wheelchair during the day to exercise. Help the student maintain muscle tone.

- Involve classmates in the care of the student. Let them help with some of the work the aid would do, such as writing for the student or taking notes.

- Assign the student to a group to work on a project, if possible without the help of the aid. Monitor the student's progress.

- Involve the student in all class activities, including field trips.

- Ensure that the student is part of the social fabric of the class.

- Talk to the parents and special education teacher about obtaining special equipment such as pencil holders, adaptive typewriters, small weights for strengthening muscles, communication aids, book holders and adjustable tables with lip rims.

Students with Epilepsy

Definition

Epilepsy is a disruption in the movement of electrical impulses through normal brain passages, which results in two degrees of seizures:

1. tonic clonic (previously called "gran mal") – a type of seizure caused by large and uncontrolled amounts of electrical energy in the brain resulting in symptoms which may last for several minutes and include loss of consciousness, convulsions, salivation, yelling, jerky movements, loss of bladder control and collapse, possibly followed by feelings of drowsiness, difficulty breathing, loss of color, or inability to remember what happened;

2. absence seizures (previously called "petit mal") – a less severe type of seizure lasting 5 to 30 seconds and caused by smaller amounts of uncontrolled electrical energy in the brain, resulting in symptoms that may occur several times a day, which include staring or smiling (appearance of day-dreaming), droopy head, jerky movements, twitching arms and shoulders, rolling eyes, or no reaction to dropping an object.

Important Facts about Students with Epilepsy

- People experiencing tonic clonic seizures are not at risk of swallowing their tongue.

- Some students experience a sensation called an "aura" which tells them when a seizure is coming.

Suggestions for Working with a Student with Epilepsy

- With the parents, school nurse and the student prepare a procedure for when a seizure occurs.

- If a student takes seizure medication ensure daily that it is being taken as prescribed.

- If a student experiences auras plan a procedure and safe place for the student to lie down, if one should occur.

- Watching a tonic clonic seizure can be very frightening. Inform the class about what to expect if the student has a seizure. Assign responsibilities to the class members, such as informing the office, moving furniture out of the way, or going for the nurse.

- In case of a tonic clonic seizure (a) protect the student from nearby hazards, (b) if possible remove the student's eyeglasses and loosen the student's collar or tie, (c) if possible place a jacket or pillow under the student's head, (d) if possible turn the student on the side to clear airways, (e) do not place anything in the student's mouth, (f) do not try to hold the student's tongue, (g) do not try to give the student liquids during or immediately after the seizure, and (h) when the seizure ends allow the student to rest and reassure the student and the class that everything is all right.

- In case of an absence seizure there is no need for the teacher to do anything but be aware of the seizure and assure the student that everything is all right.

Students with Muscular Conditions

Students with Juvenile Rheumatoid Arthritis

Definition

Juvenile rheumatoid arthritis is a condition affecting the tissue lining of the joints causing them to become painful and stiff.

Important Facts about
Students with Juvenile Rheumatoid Arthritis

- Juvenile rheumatoid arthritis can also affect the heart, liver and spleen.

- Juvenile rheumatoid arthritis can be temporary or permanent.

- The condition is commonly treated with special exercise, heat treatment and aspirin to ease the pain. In addition, some children wear casts, splints, or braces.

- A student with juvenile rheumatoid arthritis must use common sense to determine in which classroom and gym activities they can participate.

- Because it seems so difficult for a student with juvenile rheumatoid arthritis to do things alone, there is a danger of helping the student too much. It is important to let such students take care of themselves as much as possible so they have the opportunity to grow and mature as other students do.

Suggestions for Working with a Student with Juvenile Rheumatoid Arthritis

- Provide the student with adaptive materials for writing, such as a pen holder.

- Allow the student to move around periodically to prevent stiffness.

- Accommodate the student's requirement for frequent exercise.

- Encourage the best posture possible.

- Avoid prolonged physical activity, especially writing.

- Allow the student additional time to move from room to room.

- Allow the student additional time to finish written assignments.

- If a student is having difficulty writing, assign a buddy to write for him or to take an extra set of notes using carbon paper.

- Be aware that the student may have some eye problems related to the arthritis.

- Be aware that the student may be in pain and can become touchy as a result.

- Be aware that some students will have pain from moving around and should be required to move only when necessary.

Students with Muscular Dystrophy

Definition

Muscular dystrophy is a group of progressive diseases causing weakness of the voluntary muscles.

Important Facts about Students with Muscular Dystrophy

- During the early phases of the disease, muscular dystrophy may affect balance, causing the student to fall over and have difficulty running and climbing stairs.

- The ability to walk will eventually be lost.

- The student will become prone to diseases, which are usually fatal, and common infections.

- Schooling is often disrupted by hospital stays and days spent at home.

Suggestions for Working with a Student with Muscular Dystrophy

- Remain flexible working around the student's absences.

- Emphasize the quality of life over keeping up with schoolwork.

- Model a good relationship with the student and encourage the class to maintain friendships with the student.

- Realize that the student is likely to be depressed, but encourage the student to participate in classroom activities.

Students with Spinal Cord Injuries

Definition

Spinal cord injuries are accidental injuries to the spinal cord which are often the result of an automobile accident, sports accident or gunshot wound.

Important Facts about Students with Spinal Cord Injuries

- The extent of the student's disability is determined by the amount of damage and location of the injury. The higher the damage on the spinal cord, the more the body will be affected.

- The student is likely to experience problems, such as breathing difficulty, lack of bladder control, skin irritations, or sexual dysfunction.

- The student is likely to experience emotional problems associated with losing the old lifestyle and adapting to a more limited one.

Suggestions for Working with a Student with Spinal Cord Injuries

- Attempt to keep the student's life as normal as possible.

- Encourage the student's classmates to continue friendships even if they become difficult to maintain.

- Allow the student to be depressed but encourage the student to adjust to the new situation.

- Help the student to feel connected to others.

- Focus on the positive.

Glossary

ataxia – a lurching walking gait

atonia – lack of muscle tone

colostomy – a surgical opening into the abdomen to remove the bowels

congenital – present at birth

hypertonia – tightness in a muscle or muscle group

incontinence – the inability to control the bowels

jejunum tube – a tube inserted in the small intestine to provide feeding

meningocele – a serious form of spina bifida in which the covering of the spinal cord protrudes through the spine

monoplegia – paralysis of one limb

myelomeningocele – a serious form of spina bifida in which the spinal cord covering and part of the spinal cord or nerve roots protrude through the spine

myolonic seizure – a partial epileptic seizure which usually occurs in infants

orthosis – a brace used to support or align a physical deformity

paralysis – the loss of power and feeling to a part of the body

paraplegia – the impairment and limited use of the limbs

partial seizure – an epileptic seizure which affects only part of the brain

perinatal – the time from the twentieth week of pregnancy to the twenty-eighth day after birth *postnatal* – the time from the twenty-eighth day of life onward

prenatal – the time from conception to birth

prosthesis – an artificial limb

quadriplegia – a weakness in both arms and both legs

safe place – a small room or area of a classroom, prepared with a sofa or large pillows and away from outside stimuli, where a student can go during symptomatic episodes

scoliosis – a curvature of the spine

shunt – a tube implanted in the body to draw off excessive fluids

spasticity – abnormally high muscle tension which causes lack of coordination

tracheostomy – a surgical opening in the wind pipe (trachea) into which a tube is inserted to assist breathing

Reference Books

Dormans, Paul and Louis Pellegrino. *Caring for Children with Cerebral Palsy: A Team Approach.* Baltimore, MD: Paul H. Brookes, 1997.

Ratto, Linda Lee. *Coping with Being Physically Challenged.* New York, NY: Rosen, 1991.

Sandler, Adrian. *Living with Spina Bifida.* Chapel Hill, NC: University of North Carolina Press, 1997.

Van Hasselt, V., P. Strain, and M. Herson, eds. *Handbook of Developmental and Physical Disabilities.* New York, NY: Pergamon Press, 1988.

Web Sites

ABLE.net
  www.able.net.sdu.edu/ablenet.html

Association for Spina Bifida and Hydrocephalus
  www.asbah.demon.co.uk

AZ RSA Links
  www.azrsa.org/links

National Center for Youth with Disabilities (NCYD)
www.peds.umn.edu/centers/ihd

National Spinal Cord Injury Hotline, Inc.
members.aol.com/SCIHOTLINE

Chapter XIV

Students with Other Health Impairments

- *Students with Asthma*
- *Students with Juvenile Diabetes*
- *Students with Cystic Fibrosis*
- *Students with Cancer*
- *Students with HIV or AIDS*
- *Students with Birth Defects*
- *Students Who Have Been Abused*
- *Students with Cardiovascular Problems*
- *Students with Hemophilia*
- *Students with Hyperventilation*
- *Students with Severe Burns*

Definition

[Other health impairments include] having limited strength, vitality, or alertness due to chronic or acute health problems such as a heart condition, tuberculosis, rheumatic fever, nephritis, asthma, sickle cell anemia, hemophilia, epilepsy, lead poisoning, leukemia, or diabetes that adversely affect a child's educational performance. —IDEA

Important Facts about Students with Health Impairments

• The mental ability of most students is not affected by health impairments.

• However, the lack of energy (strength, vitality and alertness) or frequent absences may limit the student's ability to produce.

Suggestions for Working with a Student with Health Impairments

• The teacher should, as much as possible, keep the student with the rest of the class.

• Meet with the student, parents and school nurse. Discuss any medical procedures that must take place in school. Determine who should perform the procedures, and accept responsibility for only those you are comfortable performing. Devise a plan of action should a medical problem arise. Decide if anything should be told to the other students about the medical problem and who should tell them.

Students with Asthma

Definition

Asthma is a chronic obstructive lung condition which can vary in intensity from mild to life threatening.

Important Facts about Students with Asthma

• Asthma is triggered by allergens in the air, such as pollen, dust, mold, and animal hair.

• Stress will not cause an asthma attack, but an asthma attack can cause stress.

- Cold weather and breathing cold air can trigger an asthma attack.

- Mental exercises, which help prevent the air passages from constricting, may alleviate an asthma attack. They are, however, only meant to give partial relief until medication can be taken.

- The most common treatment for asthma is medication taken through an inhaler. The teacher may be asked to keep the student's inhaler or an extra inhaler.

Characteristic Behavior of Students with Asthma

- Exhibit chronic breathing difficulties, such as wheezing, rasping, coughing and gasping for breath.

- Periodically absent from school when breathing becomes too difficult.

Suggestions for Working with a Student with Asthma

- As much as possible treat the student like any other student.

- Do not allow the student to become a victim of his asthma.

- Do not allow the student to use the threat of an asthma attack to control the teacher or classroom activities.

- Ask the parents to inform you of any necessary restrictions on the student's activities. In PE do not exclude the student entirely, rather find some means of participation.

- If you are asked to decide when the student needs the inhaler request detailed written instructions from the parents.

- If you are asked to monitor the student's breathing with a peak flow meter, request detailed information from the parents or school nurse.

Students with Juvenile Diabetes

Definition

Juvenile diabetes is a disorder of metabolism caused by insufficient amounts of insulin produced by the body. The condition is lifelong and cannot be cured but can be controlled through proper diet, exercise and insulin shots.

If treated improperly one of two conditions may occur:

1. hyperglycemia (also known as diabetic coma) – a very serious condition resulting from insufficient insulin in the body, which can cause the student to lapse into a coma. Symptoms may include fatigue, thirst, trouble breathing, hot and dry skin, or blurred vision. Onset is slow. Hyperglycemia is usually caused by stress, excessive carbohydrates, or missed insulin injections. If the symptoms occur, a doctor or school nurse should be called immediately, and the parents notified. The student should be kept lying down and warm until medical help arrives.

2. hypoglycemia (also known as diabetic shock) – a serious condition, though less serious than hyperglycemia, resulting from too much insulin in the body which can result in convulsions or loss of consciousness. Symptoms may include dizziness, sweating, headaches, blurred vision, facial pallor, hunger, weakness, fainting, trembling, heavy heart beat, drowsiness, and confused thinking. Onset is rapid. Hypoglycemia is caused by too much physical activity, an overdose of insulin, or insufficient eating. If symptoms occur, the student should be given fruit or a drink with a high sugar content, and the symptoms should subside within 10 to 15 minutes. The parents should be notified immediately after the incident. If the student convulses or becomes unconscious due to diabetic shock, do not give the student any food or liquid. Call the school nurse or doctor immediately.

Important Facts about Students with Juvenile Diabetes

- This disorder requires a great deal of personal involvement from the student. People with diabetes tend to be more aware and involved with the maintenance of their health than any other medical disorder group.

- The student is the best manager of the disorder.

- Every student reacts to hyperglycemia and hypoglycemia differently and probably knows their particular symptoms.

- The student may have to be excused from class or classwork to take periodic blood glucose tests or to administer insulin shots.

Suggestions for Working with a Student with Juvenile Diabetes

- Treat the student like everyone else, unless the student is specifically prohibited from specific activities.

- Determine the role you are expected to play in the maintenance of the student's health.

- Be aware of the foods the student may not eat.

- Learn the student's particular hyperglycemia and hypoglycemia symptoms.

- Maintain an awareness of the student's appearance and activity.

- Expect to be asked to keep a bottle of fruit drink in your desk in case of a hypoglycemia incident.

- Allow the student to go to the washroom whenever requested.

- Allow the student to exercise at appropriate times and places.

Students with Cystic Fibrosis

Definition

Cystic fibrosis is a progressive disorder characterized by damage to the lungs, abnormal mucus production, and poor absorption of protein and fat. Damage to the lungs results in an inadequate supply of oxygen and eventual heart damage caused by the lack of oxygen.

Important Facts about Students with Cystic Fibrosis

- Students with cystic fibrosis are subject to lung infections, pneumonia and collapsed lungs.

- Students with cystic fibrosis may require physical therapy, perhaps daily, to loosen the mucus secretions in the lungs.

- Associated digestive problems require such students to take vitamin and enzyme supplements and antibiotics to fight off frequent infections.

- Those afflicted with the disease usually die by the age of twenty.

Characteristic Behavior of Students with Cystic Fibrosis

- Lack energy.

- May be in pain.

- May have frequent and lengthy absences from school.

Suggestions for Working with a
Student with Cystic Fibrosis

- Allow the student to go to the washroom whenever requested.

- Allow the student to refrain, whenever necessary, from participating in an activity.

- Maintain an area where the student can rest and lie down.

- Prepare lessons that can be taken home or to the hospital during long absences.

Students with Cancer

Definition

Cancer is a condition in which a cell or group of cells escape the controls which regulate their growth, begin to spread, and disrupt the body's normal functions.

Important Facts about Students with Cancer

- The severity of the condition and the ability to participate in class activities varies with the individual.

- Mortality rates due to cancer are decreasing as science and medicine advance. In 1965 the survival rate for people with cancer and leukemia was four percent. In 1995 in was about 72 percent.

- A student with cancer will probably undergo therapy and treatment during school time necessitating frequent absences.

- Chemotherapy treatments lower the white blood cell count and make patients more prone to infections and illnesses.

- Chemotherapy often causes hair loss. Students with hair loss are often subject to teasing from their classmates.

Characteristic Behavior of Students with Cancer

- May develop some learning disabilities if receiving cranial radiation.

- May display signs of anger and depression if receiving extensive therapy and treatment.

Suggestions for Working with a Student with Cancer

- Determine with the parents and the student whether the class should be told of the student's situation.

- Allow the student to go to the washroom whenever requested.

- Allow the student to take periodic rests. Maintain an area where the student can rest and lie down if necessary.

- Encourage the class to include the student in all activities.

- Do not allow classmates to tease a student who is experiencing hair loss due to chemotherapy.

- Allow the student to express feelings of anger and depression. However, the student should not be allowed to take out feelings on classmates.

- During sustained absences encourage the student's classmates to maintain relationships with the student.

Students with HIV or AIDS

Definitions

Human immunodeficiency virus (HIV) is a viral disease that breaks down the body's immune system making it vulnerable to invasion of other viruses.

Acquired immune deficiency syndrome (AIDS) is the final stage of HIV.

Important Facts about Students with AIDS

- Children born with HIV may not develop symptoms until they are two to five years old.

- Common symptoms in the middle stages of AIDS are fatigue, fever, night sweats, chronic diarrhea, reoccurring vaginal yeast infections, swollen glands, and frequent illnesses and infections.

- Pain is often a factor in AIDS. Death is always a factor.

- People do not die from AIDS, but from AIDS related illnesses.

- AIDS is contagious though is thought to be passed only through blood and some other bodily secretions. At this point there is no indication that HIV or AIDS is passed through kissing, swimming, sneezing or being in proximity of a person infected with AIDS.

- AIDS is controversial and communities often ostracize those who have it.

- Physicians are not required to report HIV infected people to the schools until the AIDS stage is reached.

- Children with AIDS are guaranteed public education and are considered handicapped. However, should the child present a danger to others, (i.e., having open sores or a penchant for biting) the child may be excluded as a health risk.

- Frequently changing laws and court decisions effect the way schools serve students with AIDS. Schools should periodically bring their staff up to date on the latest policies, especially when a student with AIDS is about to enroll.

Characteristic Behavior of Students with AIDS

- May be in pain.
- Lack energy.
- Frequently absent.

Suggestions for Working with a Student with AIDS

- Provide a great deal of moral support because the student may be ostracized by many.

- Show compassion for the student and teach the student's classmates to do the same.

- Teach the class about the myths and realities of AIDS. Teach appropriate life procedures for preventing the spread of AIDS.

- Learn the universal precautions regarding cleanliness before working with a student with AIDS.

- Expect the student to develop diverse and frequent illnesses.

- When necessary prepare lessons that can be taken home or to the hospital during long absences.

- During long absences keep the student and class connected by the exchange of notes, photos, phone calls and visits.

- Because of some of the uncertainties that remain concerning AIDS, it is difficult to demand that a teacher fully support the inclusion of a student with AIDS in the classroom. Regardless of your past assumptions, you should be sympathetic and professional.

- Because of possible strong opinions expressed at home, it may be difficult to demand that the students fully support the inclusion of a student with AIDS. You must at least protect the student from scorn and derision.

Students with Birth Defects

Definition

Congenital malformations (birth defects) are abnormalities that occur when the mother ingests or comes in contact with substances that harm the fetus or when the fetus becomes malformed for other reasons. The main causes of birth defects are

1. fetal alcohol syndrome (FAS) – a condition resulting from the mother drinking excessive amounts of alcoholic beverages while pregnant. The physical effects on the child may include slow growth development; facial deformities such as drooping eye lids, wide nose, flattened mid-face; seizures; cerebral palsy; microcephalia; congenital heart disease; and mild or moderate mental retardation. The behavioral and cognitive effects on the child may include acting-out behavior, language delays, attention deficits, easy overstimulation, propensity to test limits, poor peer relationships, difficulties with organization, and difficulties with problem solving

2. prenatal substance abuse – a condition resulting from the mother ingesting illegal drugs while pregnant. The effects on the child may include language delays, attention prob-

lems and a variety of physical problems. These problems may be exacerbated by the economic and environmental conditions of the mother.

3. misused drugs – a condition resulting from the mother, ingesting, while pregnant, a prescribed drug (such as thalidomide) for a medical purpose that inadvertently harms the fetus. The effects on the child are numerous and varied. They include mental retardation, missing limbs, heart problems, and deformed limbs and facial features.

4. accidental birth defects – an incomplete or improperly formed part of the body or a body system that develops before birth. The effects on the child are varied. Most common conditions are cleft palate, club foot, discrepancy in length of arms or legs, congenital hip dislocation, scoliosis, missing limbs or missing digits.

Important Facts about Students with Birth Defects

- Children subjected to prenatal substance abuse can have many problems beginning at birth; addictive substances in their blood stream can immediately cause painful withdrawals after birth.

- Not every child born to a mother who abused drugs will show deficits.

- Students who have been born with accidental defects, particularly a cleft palate, are subject to teasing from their classmates.

- In some states the legal establishment wants to make prenatal substance abuse a criminal offense.

Suggestions for Working with a Student with Birth Defects

- If the defect has not affected the student's intelligence, assign the student the same work as the rest of the class.

- If the defect has affect the student's intelligence and the student has mental retardation, follow the guidelines in Chapter VI – Students with Mental Retardation.

- Help and encourage the student to explain the birth defect to the other students, who may be inquisitive.

- Because students with birth defects are subject to teasing, the teacher should model good behavior and insist on tolerance from the rest of the class.

- Include the student in the social fabric of the class.

- Build self-esteem.

Students Who Have Been Abused

Definition

Parental child abuse is excessive physical or emotional abuse, sexual abuse or neglect which will cause physical or emotional damage to the child.

Important Facts about Students Who Have Been Abused

- Laws about reporting child abuse differ from state to state and are often revised. Schools should keep their teachers current on the necessary procedures for reporting cases of child abuse and should establish their own appropriate procedure.

- Laws and enforcement of laws about physical child abuse are vague in reference to the amount of corporal punishment parents can give their children. Usually the parents are not charged with criminal offenses unless they inflict serious harm to a child. Even in such cases the state may be reluctant to act against the parent because the prevailing philosophy among the states' family and children departments is to keep the child with the natural parents whenever possible.

- Parents who shake their babies violently may cause serious brain damage, known as shaken baby syndrome. For working with these children see Chapter XI – Students with Traumatic Brain Injury.

- Verbal child abuse is not against the law.

- Children who have been subject to child abuse may have central nervous system damage or traumatic brain injury. Physical damage may cause the child to be shorter and thinner than average. Psychological damage may cause excessive withdrawal, fear, aggression, inability to trust others, destructive behavior, school failure, or alcohol and drug abuse.

- Child abuse is a difficult problem to diagnose and usually requires a bond of trust between the teacher and the student. The student may volunteer information, or the teacher may suspect an abusive situation and ask the student for information.

Characteristic Behavior of Students Who Have Been Abused

- Often have bruises, burns, bite marks or swelling on arms, legs or torso.

- Prefer to be alone.

- May be withdrawn and secretive.

- May be aggressive and engage in rough play with classmates.

- Shrink when an adult passes closely.

- Resist informing parents about school and school behavior.

Suggestions for Working with a Student Who Has Been Abused

- If a student reports being the victim of abuse always follow school procedure in reporting it to the proper person in the building.

- Do not try to minimize the problem or talk the student out of discussing it. If you are uncomfortable in the role of listener, take (do not send) the student to a school counselor or other adult in the building who can handle the situation.

- In reporting an incident of child abuse to the proper administrator or counselor, report only what you know, not what you suspect.

- If you witness child abuse in school, you must report it.

- Do not try to intervene in family problems beyond giving moral support to the student.

Students with Cardiovascular Problems

Definition

Cardiovascular problems are problems caused by improper formation or damage to the heart.

Important Facts about
Students with Cardiovascular Problems

- Cardiovascular problems are usually congenital or acquired as a result of rheumatic fever or rubella.

Characteristic Behavior of
Students with Cardiovascular Problems

- Have frequent and prolonged absences from school.

- May be restricted from some physical activities.

Suggestions for Working with a
Student with Cardiovascular Problems

- Be flexible about keeping the student up to date with classwork.

- Have work prepared to be taken home in the event of a prolonged absence.

Students with Hemophilia

Definition

Hemophilia is a serious and potentially life-threatening condition in which the blood is unable to clot.

Important Facts about Students with Hemophilia

- Genetic testing and medical intervention have been able to greatly reduce the incidence of hemophilia.

Characteristic Behavior of Students with Hemophilia

- Will be restricted from some school activities.

- Will have absences from school if an injury occurs.

Suggestions for Working with a Student with Hemophilia

- Be constantly aware of the activities in which the student is engaged.

- Make the student's classmates aware of the medical problems the student has and the necessity of avoiding rough play.

149

- With the student's parents and the school nurse work out a plan of action in the event the student has an injury.

- Have work prepared to be taken home in the event of a prolonged absence.

Students with Hyperventilation

Definition

Hyperventilation is a condition most often caused by over-excitement, resulting in too much oxygen in the blood system.

Important Facts about Students with Hyperventilation

- There is no need to alter any work or provide any services for a student who hyperventilates, other than to treat the incidents of hyperventilation.

- Incidents of hyperventilation can be controlled by the student by being aware of when breathing is too hard.

Characteristic Behavior of Students with Hyperventilation

- Breathe rapidly.

- Become flushed.

- Become dizzy.

- May faint or lose balance and fall down.

Suggestions for Working with a Student with Hyperventilation

- Have the student lie face up. Place an open paper lunch bag over the student's mouth. Have the student breathe in and out of the bag. As the student breathes the recycled air, the amount of oxygen in the blood stream will be reduced, and the student will be able to gain full consciousness and resume classwork.

- Report all incidents of hyperventilating to the parents.

Students with Severe Burns

Definition

Severe burns are those resulting in severe scarring and disfigurement, usually to the face and hands.

Important Facts about Students with Severe Burns

- The physical results of severe burning can be alleviated or corrected by surgery. However, the surgery is usually extensive requiring several medical procedures.

Characteristic Behavior of Students with Severe Burns

- May be in pain.
- May be ostracized or may withdraw from others due to scarring and disfigurement.

Suggestions for Working with a Student with Severe Burns

- Before the student enters the class, discuss with the class what the student looks like and try to get the class to accept the student.
- If particular classmates cannot accept the student, insist they not do anything cruel.
- Model good relations with the student.
- Be flexible about keeping the student up to date with classwork.
- Have work prepared to take home in the event of a prolonged absence.

Glossary

acute – developing quickly with intense symptoms

amniotic band syndrome – a condition resulting from fibrous bands of the placenta restricting the growth of the fetus

asymptomatic – not showing any symptoms (see latency stage)

chronic – developing slowly, lasting long and often returning

crack cocaine – a type of cocaine which has been treated to make it produce greater euphoria

latency stage – a period when an infection is not causing any symptoms (see asymptomatic)

muscle atrophy – the wasting away of muscle tissue due to disease or disuse

opportunistic infection – an infection which will attack only people with HIV

respiratory ventilation – a procedure for suctioning off mucus through a small tube

service dog – a dog which has been specially trained to assist those with health impairments

T4 immune cells – the blood cells which fight infections and are a major target of HIV

Reference Books

Brotherson, M. J., L. Goldfarb, J. A. Summers, and A. Turnbull. *Meeting the Challenge of Disability or Chronic Illness - A Family Guide.* Baltimore, MD: Paul H. Brookes, 1986.

Krementz, Jill. *How Does It Feel to Fight for Your Life.* Boston, MA: Little, Brown and Co., 1989.

Web Sites

Cancer Kids
   www.cancerkids.org

Countdown for Kids (Juvenile Diabetes Foundation)
   www.jdfcure.com/cdk_001.htm

Epilepsy Foundation
   www.efa.org

The Medinex AIDS/HIV Discussion Board
   www.medinex.com/aids-hiv.shtml

Chapter XV

Students with Terminal Illnesses

- *Students Who Are Dying*
- *Death of a Student*

Students Who Are Dying

Important Facts about Students Who Are Dying

- To have a student whose death is imminent is one of the most difficult tasks a teacher can encounter. Although everyone is aware of the approaching death, the student is best served when viewed as going on like every other child in class. The dying student, especially during a time of depression, may question this practice. "Why bother learning algebra when I'll soon be dead?" Perhaps the best answer is "Because you are alive now and this is what alive people do."

- There is a tendency to move away from and not become attached to people who are dying.

- Most school boards and several organizations, especially those related to a specific illness, offer information and counseling to help people cope with the imminent death of a school friend.

Suggestions for Working with Students Who Are Dying

- Guard against moving away emotionally because the student will sense it and feel rejected.

- If the class knows of the student's impending death, always be aware that the students will be looking to you to see how they should act with the dying student.

- Consider working with the school counselor or an outside counselor to help the class understand what is taking place and how to cope with it.

- Answer questions the class may have. Discuss their concerns honestly and in terms they can understand.

- Alert the other students' parents of the situation so they can answer their children's questions and comments at home.

- If the student has been hospitalized or is having a long stay at home, encourage the class to write letters, draw pictures, and send photos and videos if the parents feel it is appropriate. If possible have the student send notes and pictures to the class.

- Realize that the student's quality of life is more important than the maintenance of schoolwork.

- Give the student art and creative writing assignments which can be left for family, friends and classmates as a legacy.

Death of a Student

Important Facts about the Death of a Student

- The death of a student is a very big loss that is difficult for class-mates, particularly young ones, to understand. It is also extremely difficult for a teacher, who is thrust into the role of being the strength of the class at a time of personal loss and vul-nerability.

- Some schools automatically send grief counselors to the classroom.

- It is all right to cry in front of the class when grieving for a lost student (this includes male teachers).

- Many children have no previous experience with death and do not know what to do. The teacher becomes a model of appropri-ate behavior.

- The children may ask to do some writing or artwork in honor of the student who has died. They may request that these works be given to the student's family.

Suggestions for Working with the Class after the Death of a Student

- In spite of your own grief, try to be with the class at this time.

- Cry in front of the class if you feel the need but do not break down completely—the children would feel the need to take care of you. If you feel unable to be in charge of the class, request cov-erage until you are able to take over again.

- If desired request that a counselor come to the room to give support. Allow the children to make comments freely and ask questions. Give answers honestly and in terms the students understand.

- If you prefer to be the only adult with the students, request that the school refrain from sending a counselor.

- Discontinue regular classwork and assign appropriate activities to help the children grieve.

- Allow individual students to leave the class with another adult if they want to have a private talk or be away from the other students.

- Notify all parents of the death and the students' reactions.

- Ask the student's family if they would like to have the class-mates at the service, burial, or after-funeral visitation. Tell the students the family's wishes and ask the class to honor them. Unless otherwise requested, go to pay your respects to the family.

- If the student's classmates are attending a service, tell them how to dress, what to expect, and what to say and do. Ask several parents to attend with their children.

- If the students decide to do something in honor of the deceased student, such as paint a mural or plant a tree, invite the student's family to attend. It will be meaningful if the family is given a collection of writings, poems, or pictures from the class.

- Watch for the individual class members who seem to be having difficulty resolving the death. Notify the children's parents and the school counselor.

- Be aware of your own feelings. Talk to someone, particularly a school colleague.

Reference Books

Cassini, Kathleen, and Jacqueline Rogers. *Death and the Classroom.* Cincinnati, OH: Griefwork of Cincinnati, 1990.

Fitzgerald, Helen. *The Grieving Child—A Parent's Guide, A Fireside Book.* New York, NY: Simon and Schuster, 1992.

Shapiro, Ester R. *Grief as a Family Process.* New York, NY: The Guilford Press, 1994.

Webb, Nancy Boyd, ed. *Helping Bereaved Children.* New York, NY: The Guilford Press, 1993.

Web Sites

Kelasan Inc.
www.death–dying.com/help.html

Index

ABLE.net, 134
absence seizures, 129, 130
abuse, child, 147–8, 151–2
acceleration, *defin.*, 75
accents, 79, 82
acquired blindness, 97; *defin.*, 102
acquired brain injury, *defin.*, 111
acquired hearing loss, *defin.*, 90
Acquired immune deficiency syndrome (AIDS), 143–5, 151–2
acting-out behavior, 15, 32, 54, 87, 145
acute, *defin.*, 151
AD/HD. *See* attention deficit/hyperactive disorder
adjustment disorder, 31
administration. *See* principal
affective disorders, 24
affective flattening, *defin.*, 121
aggressive behavior, 25, 28–9, 31, 32, 35, 37, 148
agitation, of autistic student, 54–5
aid. *See* teacher's aid
AIDS, 143–5, 151–2
albinism, *defin.*, 102
alogia, *defin.*, 121
American Foundation for the Blind, 103
American Printing House for the Blind, 103
American Psychiatric Association, 36
American Sign Language (ASL), 92; *defin.*, 91
American–Speech–Language–Hearing Association, 84, 92
Americans with Disabilities Act, *defin.*, 6
amniotic band syndrome, 119; *defin.*, 151
amphetamines, 46
anecdotal material, 3

anencephaly, *defin.*, 65
anger, of student with: AD/HD 44; BD/ED, 26; blindness, 97, 100; traumatic brain injury, 107; of teacher, 29
anorexia, 31, 32
anti-depressants, 45
anti-social personality disorder, 35
anxiety disorders, 24, 31, 35, 36, 80; and AD/HD, 41
aphasia, 12, 108; *defin.*, 83
ARC of the USA, 66
art skills, of visually impaired, 101
arthritis, juvenile rheumatoid, 130–1, 133–5
articulation: *defin.*, 83; disorders, 78
ASL, 91, 92
Asperger Disorder, *defin.,* 55
assignments, for student with: AD/HD, 41, 43, 44; autism, 52, 54; learning disability, 16–7, 19; mental retardation, 60, 62; traumatic brain injury, 109; visual impairment, 99, 101
Association for Spina Bifida and Hydrocephalus, 134
asthma, 138–9, 151–2
astigmatism, *defin.*, 102
asymptomatic, *defin.*, 151
at-risk, *defin.,* 6
ataxia, 127; *defin.*, 133
atonia, *defin.*, 133
attention, lack of, 12, 18, 107, 145
attention deficit/hyperactive disorder, 36, 40–7
audiogram, *defin.*, 90
audiologist, *defin.*, 90
augmentative communication, *defin.*, 121
aura, 129

class, 155; guilt, 59; recognizing learning disabilities, 12–3; working with an aid, 3; workload, 2–3, 114, 115, 120, 138
classwork. *See* assignments
clean intermittent catheterization (CIC), *defin.*, 121
cleft palate, 146; *defin.*, 83
club foot, 126, 146
cochlear implant, 86; *defin.*, 90
cognitive ability, of learning disabled, 12, 14
cognitive training, *defin.*, 111
color blindness, *defin.*, 102
color-coding, 19, 41
colostomy, *defin.*, 133
coma, diabetic, 140
communication board, 54, 116, 120
communication disorders, 78–84, 120; *defin.*, 78
communication skills: of autistic students, 50, 52, 54
compacting, *defin.*,75
computer skills, 16, 17, 42, 52, 60, 72, 89
conceptualization, *defin.*, 75
conduct disorder, 32
conductive hearing loss, *defin.*, 90
congenital, *defin.*, 133
congenital anomaly, 126
congenital blindness, *defin.*, 102
congenital hearing loss, *defin.*, 90
congenital malformations, 145–7, 151–2
contingency contracting, 36
contracts, behavioral, 41
convergent thinking, *defin.*,75
coordination, of learning disabled, 15
Council on Education of the Deaf, 92
Countdown for Kids , 152
crack cocaine, *defin.*, 152
creativity, *defin.*, 75
cross-eyed, *defin.*, 102

crying in front of class, 155
cued speech, *defin.*, 92
Cylert, 45; *defin.*, 46
cystic fibrosis, 141–2, 151–2

Daily Apple, The, 21
daydreaming, 42
deaf culture: *defin.*, 90; view of cochlear implant, 86
Deaf World Web, 93
deafness, 86–7, 89–93; *defin.*, 86
decibel, *defin.*, 90
delusions, 117; *defin.*, 121
depressant, 46
depression, 24, 30, 31, 32, 118, 132; of student with: AD/HD 41; terminal illness, 154
destructive behavior, 26, 30, 32
developmental disability, *defin.*, 65
Dexedrine, *defin.*, 45
diabetes, juvenile, 139–41, 151–2
diabetic retinopathy, *defin.*, 102
diagnosis: of BD/ED, 25; of AD/HD, 40
Diagnostic and Statistical Manual of Mental Disorders, *defin.*, 36
dialect, 79; *defin.*, 83
differentiated curriculum, *defin.*,75
directions, ability to follow:; for autistic students, 53; for learning disabled students, 15, 18
disability, *defin.*, 6. *See also names of specific disabilities*
disabled student. *See* student with disability
discrepancy, *defin.*, 20
divergent thinking, *defin.*, 75
Down Syndrome, 59, 65, 66
drugs: misused, 146. *See also* medication
DSM-IV, *defin.*, 36
due process, *defin.*, 6
dyscalculia, *defin.*, 20
dysgraphia, *defin.*, 20
dyskenesia, 127

(HIV), 143–5, 151–2

hyperactivity, 40, 46. *See also* attention deficit/hyperactive disorder

hyperglycemia, 140, 141

hypertonia, *defin.,* 133

hyperventilation, 150–2

hypoglycemia, 140, 141, 151–2

IDEA. *See* Individuals with Disabilities Education Act

idiot-savant, 50, 55

IEP. *See* Individual Education Plan

incontinence, 32, 121, 128; *defin.,* 133

IFSP. *See* Individualized Family Service Plan

Illinois Test of Psycholinguistic Abilities (ITPA), 12

impulsive behavior, 20, 33, 35

impulsivity, *defin.,* 46

inattentive type AD/HD, 42–3

inclusion 2–9: attitudes that ruin, *x; defin.,* 2; federal laws regarding, 2; history of, *vii–viii;* philosophy of, 2; successful elements for, *x*

independent living skills, for mentally retarded, 64

Individual Education Plan (IEP), 2–5; *defin.,* 6; of traumatic brain injured, 108; of severely or multiply disabled, 114

Individualized Family Service Plan (IFSP), *defin.,* 6

Individuals with Disabilities Education Act (IDEA), *vii, ix; defin.,* 6

inhaler, 139

inkblot test, 37

instructions, 43; from doctor or nurse, *ix,* 25; following, 41

insulin, 139–40

integrated classroom, *defin.,* 6

interdisciplinary team, *defin.,* 6

interest in school, loss of, 15, 27, 32

International Dyslexic Society, 21

interpreter, sign language, 90

I.Q., 51; high, 68, 69, 70, 72; low, 58, 115–6

islets of competence, 51

itinerant teacher, *defin.,* 7

ITPA, 12

jejunum tube, *defin.,* 133

job coach, *defin.,* 65

job training, 63

joints, painful, 130

Juvenile Diabetes Foundation, 152

juvenile rheumatoid arthritis, 130–1, 133–5

Kelasan Inc., 156

Kids Together Inc., 9

language arts skills, of mentally retarded, 61, 63

language delay, 55, 79, 145

language disorders, 78, 79

late talking, 79

latency stage, of infection, *defin.,* 152

laws, regarding child abuse, 147

lawsuit, 3

LDA, 21

L.D. Online, 21

learned helplessness, *defin.,* 65

learning disabilities: *defin.,* 12; language, 78; students with, 12–21, 36, 143

Learning Disabilities Association (LDA), 21

Learning Disabilities Professional's Directory, 21

least restrictive environment, *defin.,* 7

legally blind, 96; *defin.,* 99–100

life-skills curriculum, *defin.,* 65

lifting, 3